Unclutter Your Life in One Week

Unclutter Your Life in One Week

Erin Rooney Doland

SIMON SPOTLIGHT ENTERTAINMENT

NEW YORK LONDON TORONTO SYDNEY

Simon Spotlight Entertainment
A Division of Simon & Schuster, Inc.
1230 Avenue of the Americas
New York, NY 10020

First Simon Spotlight Entertainment hardcover edition November 2009

SIMON SPOTLIGHT ENTERTAINMENT and colophon
are trademarks of Simon & Schuster, Inc.

For information about special discounts for bulk purchases,
please contact Simon & Schuster Special Sales at 1-866-506-1949
or business@simonandschuster.com

The Simon & Schuster Speakers Bureau can bring authors to your live event.
For more information or to book an event contact the
Simon & Schuster Speakers Bureau at 1-866-248-3049
or visit our website at www.simonspeakers.com.

Designed by Diane Hobbing/SnapHaus Graphics
Illustrations by Mark Watkinson

Manufactured in the United States of America

1 3 5 7 9 10 8 6 4 2

Library of Congress Cataloging-in-Publication Data
Doland, Erin Rooney.
Unclutter your life in one week / Erin Rooney Doland.
p. cm.
1. Storage in the home.   2. Orderliness.   3. House cleaning.   I. Title.
TX309.D75 2009
648'.8—dc22

2009021841

ISBN 978-1-4391-5046-7
ISBN 978-1-4391-5420-5 (ebook)

For PJ

Contents

Foreword

We live in a culture that seems to create a lot more than it completes and collect a lot more than it cleans up. At the macro level, it's mountains of garbage that can't find a home and carbon dioxide taking over the atmosphere. On the micro side, it's the propensity of each of us to generate "stuff"—the detritus that can clog our garages, hallways, computers, and heads.

We really don't do this on purpose. No one I know wakes up and says, "I can't wait to go gather more piles of unnecessary, numbing, extraneous glop!" But it happens to the best of us. Time changes the meaning of things, so if you simply do nothing, "stuff" accumulates around you. The ballpoint refills in your drawer became useless when that pen disappeared, as well as the mementos of your boyfriend when he went with it. Keeping everything around you current and relevant is a continual challenge requiring eternal vigilance and a consistent investment of time and energy. Ninety percent of my gardening is cleanup. Denying that reality diminishes my enjoyment of its beauty.

The rewards are immense when the back end of the creative process is absorbed as habit in your endeavors—the closure, the sweep-up, the reordering of your tools. A sense of freedom, clarity, and general lightness of being accompanies an uncluttered space—in your kitchen, in your office, and in your life.

Erin Doland has experienced this from both sides, and she gives this highly practical manual for achieving that kind of positive experience an elegant dose of empathy and understanding. There are challenges. To stop accumulating clutter you'll need to move beyond irrational attachments, step out of your comfort zone, and overcome basic inertia. But Erin does a great job in taking you by the hand with step-by-step instructions that make the process not only easier than you think but fun as well. Follow her directions and you'll reap enormous benefits.

David Allen

Ojai, California

May 19, 2009

Erin's Story

"I'll need two copies of your book," my friend said.

"Two copies?" I asked. "One for you and one for a gift?"

"No, both copies for me," she explained. "I'll lose at least one in all of my crap."

I nodded my head immediately. "I know *exactly* what you mean."

Almost a decade ago, surrounded by stacks of papers, piles of shoes and clothes, and dozens of boxes of sentimental trinkets, my husband had a conversation with me that changed my life. He asked me to sit next to him, took my hand in his, and told me he could no longer live with all of my clutter. He said he wanted to build a remarkable life with me, but all of my stuff was getting in the way. There were so many of my possessions crammed, packed, and shoved into our 850-square-foot Washington, DC, apartment that we had to shuffle along a narrow path of waist-high towers of boxes to get from the bedroom to the kitchen. We were so embarrassed that we never had friends over to our place. We didn't relax when we were home, and when we were out of the apartment we felt anxious about the chaos waiting for us when we returned.

When my husband talked to me about my clutter problem he didn't threaten to leave or issue any ultimatums; instead he described what we could gain with a clutter-free life. He said he wanted a home with room for friends and family to gather, space to plan new adventures, and the opportunity to create happy memories—not a home jam-packed with possessions. He knew he couldn't force me to change, but he was asking me to try.

I told him I was up for the task and I also wanted the life he imagined. What I didn't tell him was that I had no idea *how* I was going to make any of it happen. In particular, I had no clue how I would be able to let go of so many of my things. I spent most of the next day at work devising elaborate schemes to transport my stuff to a storage facility and thinking of ways to convince him we needed to move into a larger place. I'd do whatever it took to keep my things. Those plans faded quickly, however, when on my walk home that evening I remembered the disorder that was waiting back at the apartment. My stomach knotted, I tightened my shoulder and neck muscles, and I started walking slowly. My husband was right; I had to change the way I lived.

It didn't happen in thirty minutes like it does on television, but I did change. I cleared the clutter and became organized (eventually, even becoming the editor-in-chief of Unclutterer .com). I said farewell to the mess and started living a remarkable life. I did it, and so can you.

chapter 1

Foundations

Simplicity is revolutionary.

Being overworked, overbooked, and overwhelmed is passé.

Right now, you have a choice to make. Do you want to live a stressful life controlled by your possessions and the demands of things that don't matter to you? Or do you want to be relaxed and living a remarkable, uncluttered life?

When I made the decision to live simply, it took me fewer than seven days to clear the physical clutter from my life. Unfortunately, those seven days took place sporadically over six months because I didn't have resources to guide me through the process. I wanted a manual to explain to me the *hows* and *whys* of simplifying, organizing, time management, uncluttering, and productivity—but I never found it. I've created this book so that you can unclutter your life in one week. It's going to be hard work, but you deserve to live with less stress and anxiety. You deserve a remarkable life. And, most important, you deserve to experience all the benefits of being an unclutterer.

> **Unclutterer** (un-ˈklə-tər-ər) *n.* Someone who chooses
> to get rid of the distractions that get in the way of a
> remarkable life.

Distractions, also known as clutter, come in many forms—physical, time management, mental, and bad systems. When your surroundings, schedule, and thoughts are chaotic, it's hard to move through the day. If you're constantly late to work because you're having trouble getting out the door in the morning, then you may have a problem with organization. If your house is in such disarray that you can't have friends over for dinner, then your problem is likely with physical clutter. If you are overwhelmed with e-mail at work and laundry at home, then you may be using bad processes. If you are repeatedly missing client deadlines, then you may need some time management help. The list of distractions is endless, and only *you* know specifically how clutter is interfering with your life. By getting rid of clutter and organizing your work and home life, you will free up time, space, and energy so that you can focus on what really matters to you.

As Albert Einstein explained, "Things should be made as simple as possible, but not any simpler."

An unclutterer lives as simply as he or she can without making life difficult. For instance, I love books and devote an entire wall of my living room to them, but I don't have more books than I can store on those shelves. You might enjoy television, but instead of being tied to the networks' schedules, you record programs on your DVR and watch them when it is convenient for you. Simple living isn't about depriving; it's about enriching. You're getting rid of what doesn't belong to make room for what does.

The official unclutterer motto has been passed down from generation to generation by parents, teachers, and large purple dinosaurs: *A place for everything, and everything in its place.* Nothing in your home or office should be without a designated living space. Every pair of slacks should have a hanger and space in your closet to hang without getting wrinkled. Every pen in your office should have room in a cup or a container to rest easily when not in use. Think of it this way: If Oprah were to surprise you and say your home or office was going to be featured on her show, you shouldn't have to run around tossing things into a box to get your space to look the way you want. When everything has a proper place, you never have to wonder where something is or think twice about where to put it when you're done using it. This way of living might sound like a big change for you—it certainly was for me—but you're totally capable of making it.

Why Change?

I can't force you to become an unclutterer or go through the process for you, but I can give you the tools and information you'll need to make it happen. You're in control here, and you're the one who is going to have to put in the elbow grease if you really want to make a change. The benefits of an organized life are so incredible, though, that all of the sweat you invest will be worth it.

If you think making changes in your life is difficult, you're right. Considering an actual life-and-death situation, only one in ten Americans who has had heart bypass surgery changes his lifestyle to prevent future heart attacks. Most patients don't adopt healthier lifestyles because they receive very limited information and minimal support about how to make positive changes. When patients are provided with resources and the opportunity to learn about the benefits of making significant changes to their lives, the statistic improves from 10 percent to 77 percent. Almost eight out of ten people will make significant changes to the way they live if given the proper motivation and information for success.[1]

So why am I talking about the grim realities of bypass surgery patients in a book on organizing? Good question. I mentioned these statistics because change of any kind—the life-and-death kind and the not-so-doom-threatening kind— is difficult. Scribbling "Be more organized" on a list of New Year's resolutions doesn't take much effort, but actually *becoming* an unclutterer requires change.

This book will be your support system and resource manual as you go through the process of uncluttering and organizing your life. Since I'm taking care of giving you the tools, you're going to have to supply the second ingredient of success: motivation. You need to determine why you want to make a change. What is it that will drive you to keep working even when you're struggling?

Close your eyes for a minute, take deep breaths, and let your mind fill with all the things that make you happy. I know it sounds silly, but do it anyway. Relax and focus on the good things in life.

What came into your mind? Did you see the faces of your friends and family? What were you doing? Where were you? Why did these things bring you happiness?

Now make a list of those things that came into your mind. Group items on your list that belong in the same overarching category. Family, friends, hobbies, personal time, good health, career, vacationing, and spirituality are common groups of items, but your list will be unique to your life. Also, no one but you is going to pay attention to this list, so be honest with yourself—don't list what you *think* you should list, identify what *really* makes you happy. This list is your motivation. These items are the reasons you want to become an unclutterer. This list is a reminder to you of *what matters most* in your life.

Take your list and put it somewhere easily accessible. Fold it up and put it in your wallet or tape it to the dashboard of your car. There will be times when you're ready to give up on the process and looking at this list will quickly remind you why you're making a change. This is the life you want.

One of the things on my list is travel. I want to drink wine in Bordeaux, ski the Alps in Switzerland, and photograph elephants in Thailand. To make these trips, I have to save my money and be able to clear my calendar on short notice. Budgeting my finances and juggling my work responsibilities require scheduling, time management, and planning. The more organized and uncluttered my life is, the easier it is for me to be able to travel. Experiencing the world firsthand is a powerful motivator, and so is time with my husband, family, and friends, and being able to accomplish the other items on my list. Do a bit of soul searching and figure out what and who matter most to you. What is it you wish you could do more often or with improved quality?

Work-Life Symbiosis

When people talk about what matters most and what they hope to achieve through the uncluttering process, I often hear responses that include the phrase "work-life balance." People need to work, but they want to balance that need for income with a rich personal life.

"Work-life balance" is just a buzz phrase in the business world. As far as I can tell, it exists for the sole purpose of making people feel bad. We hear the phrase "work-life balance" and like Pavlov's dog we're triggered into thinking, "Ugh, if only I had work-life balance! I would be happy if I had work-life balance! It sounds so dreamy!"

Um, it's not dreamy—it's bullshit.

Seriously, do you want your work life to sit in perfect balance with your personal life? Do you want to be at work the exact same amount of time as your free time? (And, don't forget, you spend a good portion of that free time sleeping.) Since there are 168 hours in a week, you would need to work 84 hours to keep things in "balance." To keep things equal, you wouldn't have time to enjoy the money you would be making.

Put aside the numbers for a minute and think only about the quality of your work. My guess is that you draw from experiences in your personal life to help solve problems in your work life. You remember something you encountered when you weren't at your office or from your past and it helps to spur an idea that advances your work. You can't flip a switch and immediately stop being Personal You when you're in the office fulfilling the role of Employee You. You're one person, not two, and you can't be balanced.

Stop feeling inadequate about not having "work-life balance" and accept the fact that it is unachievable and undesirable. Instead, aim for something you can attain and enjoy: work-life symbiosis.

Work-life symbiosis is what you achieve when all aspects of your life exist together harmoniously. It's as crucial to your achieving a remarkable life as simplifying, organizing, managing your time, uncluttering, maintaining your ideal level of productivity, and exploring your personal interests. In fact, the work-life symbiosis concept is the basis of how this book is organized. Explore a week of your life and see how you can smoothly transition from personal life to work life and back again. Arrive at work on time. Go hear your friend's band play on a weeknight. Fall asleep without a stream of to-do items for work the next day racing through your mind.

As you continue to create your list of what matters most and your vision of your remarkable life, keep this big-picture perspective of work-life symbiosis in mind. Avoid the buzz phrase, and decide what is most important—truly important—to you.

Questions for Your Things

Smart consumerism is another fundamental component of being an unclutterer. The more you know about the things you buy, the better the consumer you'll be. When you know what you own and what you need, you don't make impulse buys in the checkout line. You buy useful, inspiring, and well-made goods—but only when you need to.

Smart consumerism isn't something that comes naturally to me. Truthfully, I hate shopping. For years, I made horrible decisions about what I purchased because I wanted to get in and out of a store as quickly as possible. While I can't stand shopping, I know that many people struggle with the opposite of my problem—a deep love for shopping. A number of my friends have told me that they feel a rush of adrenaline when they enter a mall or a store. Even when they don't need things, they like to window-shop and imagine themselves buying things.

Thankfully, there is a middle ground between deprivation and materialism, where you can respect and care for the things you own and make informed decisions about purchases. You can be a smart consumer and maintain an uncluttered home and office. As you prepare to clear the clutter from your life, it can be beneficial to ask questions of the things that are already in your space. Just because something has made it into your home or office doesn't mean that it has to remain there. The following series of questions has helped me make informed decisions about the items I own. This list has changed with time, and I expect it to go through some adjustments as my family grows, so feel free to adapt it for your personal needs. If you make changes, though, try not to stray too far from the underlying intent of the list.

Questions for Items Already in Your Home

1. Do I have something else like this that fulfills the same purpose?

2. If this is a duplicate item, which of these items is in the best condition, of the best quality, and will last me the longest?

3. Is this item in disrepair and in need of replacing or fixing?

4. Does this item make my life easier/save me time/save me money/fulfill an essential need?

5. Why does this object live in my house, and is this the best place for this object?

6. Do I need to do more research to determine whether this is the best object to fulfill its essential need?

7. If this is a perishable item, has its expiration date passed?

8. Does this item help me to develop the remarkable life I want to live?

While uncluttering, you may even find that you need to replace damaged objects or need organizing and cleaning products. Also, there isn't anything wrong with buying things you want or need as long as you're sure they meet the following criteria.

Questions to Ask Before You Buy

1. Do I have something else like this already that fulfills the same purpose?

2. If I own something like this, am I ready to get rid of the older item since this newer item will have to replace it? (This is commonly referred to as the "one in, one out" rule.)

3. Will this item make my life easier/save me time/save me money/fulfill an essential need?

4. Where will this object live in my house?

5. Is this the best price for this object and the best quality I can get for the money?

6. Do I need to do more research about this object before I make this purchase/bring it into my home? Have I researched similar products?

7. If this is a perishable item, when will I use it and what will I do if I don't use all of it?

8. Does this item help me to develop the remarkable life I want to live?

Here's how you might work through the process:

	Toaster	Printer	Snuggie— the blanket with sleeves	Bag of candy
1. Something like this?	No, old one broke	No, old one broke	Regular blankets	No
2. Get rid of older item?	Yes	Yes	No	N/A
3. Easier/save time/save money/ fulfill need?	Need toaster to make morning toast	Need printer to print papers	No, just funny	Satisfies sweet tooth but not healthy eating plans
4. Where will it live?	Kitchen counter	On desk next to phone	On ottoman next to couch	In bowl on dining table
5. Best price and best quality?	Yes, great reviews on Amazon and CNET	Don't know	I could make one for less	Yes
6. Did I compari- son shop?	Yes	Not yet	No	No
7. Use before expires?	N/A	N/A	N/A	Maybe
8. Remarkable life?	Sure	Sure	It will make me laugh, that's it	I'll be mad at myself if I finish the bag
Final Decision	Purchase	Continue research be- fore making purchase	Do not purchase	Do not purchase

In the past, I've heard criticisms about these questions because they seem to suggest that only utilitarian items—objects that fulfill a duty and provide utility—should exist in a home or office. For some people, a utilitarian-only system might work. I wouldn't enjoy living that way, however. I need objects that also inspire me or make me laugh when I see them. These objects are able to filter into my home through question eight, which asks whether the item helps me to develop the remarkable life I want to live. Just be sure that objects that agree with question eight also pass muster with the others.

With the help of these questions, the information throughout this book, and the projects you're going to complete, you will transform into an unclutterer. Clearing the distractions will make way for a simple, efficient, symbiotic, clutter-free life. Get ready to make room for what matters most.

It's okay if some possessions made your list of what matters most. I know many knitters who would feel like someone chopped off their hands if they got rid of their favorite sets of needles. My brother loves to build race cars and would be lost without his garage of tools. An unclutterer makes room for what matters most, and if certain possessions are on that list, then get rid of clutter to make room for these objects.

Going on a Sentimental Journey

Do you keep ticket stubs after you see a movie? Do you display gifts or use items you don't like out of a sense of obligation to the person who gave them to you? Do you store bridesmaid dresses you wore in your friends' weddings, even if the couple eventually divorced? Do you have T-shirts from college parties you attended more than five years ago?

Wanting to keep sentimental objects is a natural desire, especially if the objects remind us of someone we care about or if they are associated with pleasant memories. We can't collect and keep objects associated with every happy memory over the course of our lives, though. It takes time, energy, and space to store sentimental items—and, unless possessions are on your list of what matters most, you need that time, energy, and space for more important things.

Sentimental clutter can be the hardest type to conquer. When an object offers such wonderful memories, the obvious fear is that getting rid of the object would mean losing the memory or the connection to the person who gave it to you. It's important to remember the past, but an unclutterer chooses not to live in it. Literally.

Before you start your week of uncluttering, I want you to remove the sentimental clutter from your life. Your basement, attic, off-site storage space, and/or closets are likely filled with these things. You don't have to part with everything (some of the sentimental items you have may not actually be clutter), but think about paring down what you have. When I sorted through my stuff, I found three grocery sacks of notes from middle school and high school, a pair of my grandfather's overalls, and invitations to every wedding I've ever been invited to. When viewed in terms of the questions I posed earlier, these items don't seem like they could hold much sentimentality—but they did. You'll likely find similar types of clutter in your spaces.

Remember the list of questions I recommended you ask about the items already in your home. Keep them in front of you and use them as a reference as you sort through your sentimental things. Set limits for yourself, stick to these limits, and aim for quality, not quantity.

Tips for Handling Sentimental Clutter

- *Picture Perfect.* An image of an object can be as powerful as the object itself. Take digital photographs of the items before you get rid of them. When you upload the image to your computer, type in the memory you have associated with the object into the file's "Notes" field. (For example, I had my picture taken wearing my grandfather's overalls in an alfalfa field on his farm before I repurposed the fabric.) Be sure to back up your computer's hard drive so that you don't have to worry about losing the images.

- *Simply the Best.* If you inherit a set of something like your grandmother's china, you don't have to keep all of it. Display one place setting or even just a teacup and saucer.

- *Digital Revolution.* Scan papers and pictures and turn them into digital files. It's a lot easier to store a computer hard drive than it is to keep boxes of memorabilia. Feel like you have no time to do this on your own? Hire a company for this task, like ScanMyPhotos (scanmyphotos.com) for pictures or Pixily (pixily.com) for documents.

- *Share the Wealth.* After scanning papers and pictures, give the originals away to friends and family. This is what I did with my collection of notes. Once I scanned them, I sent a few of the gems off to their original authors. My childhood friends read the notes, laughed, and then shredded the evidence. You also could throw a party where guests are instructed to take any of your old pictures they want—this is especially nice to do with family photographs at reunions.

- *Repurpose.* If your dresser is filled with T-shirts from college, cut them up and make them into a quilt. You can enjoy the warmth of the blanket all winter long and also make room in your clothes drawer.

- *Buddy Up.* Researchers at Ohio State University found that touching an item (even something as ordinary as a coffee mug) creates an emotional connection to that item, and the longer you hold it, the stronger the bond.[2] Enlist the help of a buddy to hold up items for you in order to keep the duration of exposure to a minimum and make parting with items significantly easier.

- *Pass It On.* When someone gives you a gift, it's because they want to make a connection with you and bring you happiness. Unfortunately, not all gifts are things we want. If someone gives you a gift that doesn't work with your space, say thank you and feel no guilt regifting or donating the unused object to charity. The gift giver (if he or she has any tact) won't ever ask you what you chose to do with the item. If the person does ask, respond that you don't currently have the item out on display. The person will get the hint and drop the subject, and life will continue.

- *Make It Speedy.* If the sentimental clutter is best suited for recycling or the trash, get it out of your sight as quickly as possible. Repeatedly walking past the clutter in a trash can or recycling bin will make it even harder to say good-bye.

Whatever sentimental objects you wish to keep you should display and/or use in your home. Nothing sentimental should be stuffed in a box in your basement or attic gathering dust. Why keep something that doesn't reflect the remarkable life you want to live?

When Uncluttering Goes Too Far

When I initially went through the uncluttering process, I wanted my life to be instantly clutter free. So I took a shortcut and got rid of some of my boxes of sentimental clutter without opening them and properly sorting through their contents. Since I hadn't opened the boxes in years, I assumed that there couldn't be anything I wanted or needed inside of them. This was a huge mistake. One of the boxes I blindly threw away turned out to be a box from my move that I hadn't ever unpacked. Inside of it was my passport and Social Security card.

Even if you're 99 percent sure that the box in your attic is filled with mix tapes or last-minute Halloween costumes from your childhood, take the time to look through it. Move at your own pace and reap the benefits.

chapter 2

Monday

Although calendars would have you believe that Sunday is the first day of the week, it's really Monday that starts the ball rolling. You begin the week and work toward Friday like a giant crescendo that explodes into the relaxing weekend. I love my job, and still I wish that Monday mornings weren't, well, Monday mornings. We work so that we can afford to take care of the things that matter most to us, but that doesn't mean getting out of bed and starting the week is always fun.

Research shows that if you start your week off with good routines (things like going to the gym), you're more likely to keep up the positive behavior throughout the whole of the week. If you wait to start a habit until Wednesday, you'll talk yourself out of the good behavior completely with promises that you'll start next week. Thankfully, since you are focused on achieving a remarkable life, you have the motivation to begin working to put an end to your uncluttered existence right now.

Today you need to tackle the "firsts." These are the areas you first see when you wake up, when you get to work, and when you return home in the evening—your closet, your desk, and the entryway into your home. They are also places you are guaranteed to encounter every day this week. Clearing the clutter and organizing these spaces first will repeatedly remind you of the benefits of your hard work and make the rest of your week (and your life) extremely pleasant.

Monday Morning: Your Wardrobe

The sun hasn't come up yet as you make your way to your closet to choose your clothes for the day. Your closet is a mess, and you're immediately filled with anxiety. Where are the pants that go with that jacket? Does this shirt have something on it? Why doesn't this fit? How is it my closet is full, yet I have nothing to wear? Instead of making a carefree, five-second stop on your way to get your coffee, you waste ten minutes deciding what to wear in a chaotic, stress-inducing, confined space.

There are hundreds of places in your home and office where you can begin clearing clutter, but my favorite place to start is the bedroom closet. As the first space you see when you wake up, an organized closet can be a bright spot at the start of your day.

The second reason we're starting with the bedroom closet is because physically it's a small space. Unless you live in a mansion with an enormous wing dedicated to storing your apparel, your closet probably occupies less than twenty square feet in your home. (My bedroom closet barely occupies twelve square feet.) Once your closet has been uncluttered, you will quickly see the results of your efforts and build momentum for your week of organizing.

Weeding Through Your Wardrobe

You're going to want to drive right in and start purging clutter. Don't. It's important to first get an idea of what you currently own. Wash everything in your dirty clothes hamper and pick up any items that may be at the dry cleaner. If you store your clothes in multiple locations around your home (such as a hall closet full of coats and hats or a basement closet full of formal wear), bring the stored items into your bedroom. Your first goal is to make sure that your entire wardrobe is clean and in one workspace. Seeing all of your clothes in one location can be an eye-opening experience.

Remove all inexpensive plastic bags from clothing. Stores and dry cleaners often wrap clothes in plastic bags to protect your clothes during transport. However, this plastic can damage and stain your clothes as it deteriorates. Also, remove any colorful tags a dry cleaner might use to identify your clothing. The color from the paper can bleed onto the underlying cloth. Use cotton or durable plastic garment bags intended for long-term storage if you want to store suits or formal wear in bags.

Now that you have all of your items together, it's time to answer a few questions about your clothes:

1. How do you feel about your clothes?

2. What types of clothes (work clothes, exercise clothes, formal wear) do you own?

3. Do you notice any patterns (repeated colors, styles, sizes, seasons) in your wardrobe?

Okay, I admit, question number one is a little touchy-feely. However, it is still a valid question. If you look at your clothes and feel overwhelmed by the quantity, then you know you need to get rid of a lot of stuff. If you look at your clothes and feel blah or ho-hum about what you see, then it might be time to make room for some new pieces. If you feel a sentimental attachment to your clothes, it might be harder for you to let things go, even garments you haven't worn in years.

Your answer to the second question will give you insight into where you may be able to start clearing the clutter. If you don't regularly attend formal affairs but have three tuxedos or fifteen ball gowns, then you know this will be a good area in your wardrobe to begin making space. The same applies to exercise clothes—if you don't wear them, get rid of them.

Your answer to the third question will help you establish your guidelines for what will stay in your wardrobe and what will go. As creative as you are, you still wear clothing that follows a pattern. You might notice trends of colors (my closet is completely void of jewel tones) or fabrics (almost all natural fibers) or cuts (fitted instead of baggy). Half your wardrobe might be two sizes too small, or maybe half is dedicated to a season that only lasts two months out of the year. You might even find that you've purchased the same item multiple times (which is why you need to work with your entire wardrobe all at once).

While you're collecting information about your clothing, it's also a good idea to evaluate your storage space. Remove the rest of the stuff (belts, shoes) from your closet and dresser drawers and lay it on your bed. Now, take a look at your closet. Is it in good condition? Do any repairs need to be made? Is your storage system meeting your needs? If you want to repaint, repair, dust, hang hooks, replace rods, or change your wardrobe storage in any way, do it while your closet is empty. Ultimately, your storage space determines the maximum size of your wardrobe, which is something that you'll need to keep in mind as you continue to work.

Wearing a Uniform

Clothing says a lot about who we are, regardless of whether we want it to speak for us or not. When I throw on a T-shirt and a pair of jeans, my clothing says that I'm not getting married in the next hour or heading into a suit-wearing office environment. If my T-shirt has text or an image printed on it, then I'm conveying even more information about myself. You will interpret the visual information you gain about me and make assumptions and conclusions based on your past interactions with people who look like me. Whatever those conclusions are, accurate or inaccurate, you make them based on my clothes, hygiene, posture, and outward physical appearance.

I'm not sure what kind of a message Steve Jobs intends to send with his black turtlenecks and jeans, but his look over the past decade has become as iconic as the Apple brand. The Seth Brundle character in the film *The Fly* had a similar habit of wearing the same outfit every day. Brundle said that he adopted a habit of Albert Einstein's when he bought five identical sets of clothes so as not to waste mental energy deciding what to wear each day. Einstein actually wore quite a varied wardrobe, but it's an interesting concept all the same. I believe that if I like all of the clothes in my closet and look good in them, then I don't have to waste energy deciding what to wear. I can experience the conveniences of wearing a uniform without actually wearing the same clothes every day.

You may not know exactly what you want your clothes to say about you, but you probably have a good idea what you don't want them to say. When I was in my twenties and leading a forum on school uniform policies, a group of high school students told me I dressed like a "frumpy pants." It was a few seconds after that moment that I decided I *didn't* want my clothes to say that I was a "frumpy pants."

Years later, after reading Carrie McCarthy and Danielle LaPorte's book *Style Statement,* I figured out a more proactive concept for my wardrobe choices. I've found that having a defined style has made it a lot easier to keep clutter out of my wardrobe. Nothing comes into my wardrobe that doesn't project my image.

While thinking about your own style and personal uniform, I also want you to think about the patterns you noticed in your wardrobe. Do you already have a uniform? Which clothes work for you and the image you want to project?

All of these can come together as guidelines for your wardrobe. Use the following general guidelines to decide whether a piece of clothing should be a part of your wardrobe:

1. The item should represent your current style and the image you wish to project to others.

2. The item should fit you well and complement your body shape.

3. The item should work in coordination with a minimum of two other items in your wardrobe.

4. You should be able to wear the item with shoes you already own (for shoes, you should be able to wear them with clothing you already own).

5. The item should be in good condition and should not need to be repaired.

6. There should be space for the item to be properly stored.

7. You should like how you feel when you wear the item (for shoes, they should not cause blisters).

8. You should have an occasion in the next year to wear it.

You may have additional guidelines that you wish to add to the list. I used to have a ninth guideline that said, "No orange." If you live in a tropical climate, you might consider "No sweaters." Set guidelines that are reasonable and make the most sense for you, your style/uniform, and your space.

> Extra Credit: Consider printing out your guidelines and hanging them on the back of your closet door or someplace you can easily reference them. After your wardrobe is organized, you may even want to print out a smaller version of the guidelines and a description of your style and put them in your wallet to refer to when shopping.

Closet Clearing

Purging clutter from your wardrobe may be the hardest part of this organizing project—or it could be the easiest. If you have a difficult time letting go of clothes you don't wear, bring in a trusted friend to help you at this point. Your friend can hold up clothes for you (remember that you might feel an unrealistic bond with your clothes if you touch them) and you can make decisions about each item as it is displayed. An uncluttering buddy can help to keep you on track if you get bored easily and find yourself wandering around your home instead of organizing your closet. If you work best on your own, consider playing energetic music to keep you motivated.

Start at the top of your clothes pile on your bed and work your way through your garments, sorting them into three groups: items you want to *keep,* items you want to *purge,* and items that need *extra attention,* like repairs. Look at each piece of clothing and decide which pile it belongs in based on your guidelines and your style. If you come into contact with an item and are having trouble making a decision, put it in your *keep* pile for now. You'll have to go through this pile again when you put the clothes back into your closet, so you will have another opportunity to decide to purge the item.

Do you have three blue oxford shirts? Do you need all three of them? If you only have room and need for one blue oxford shirt, keep the one that has the most versatility in your wardrobe (guidelines 3 and 4) and that people always compliment you on when you're wearing it (guidelines 2 and 7). Do you have four black turtlenecks? Are they all still black, or have some become a greenish-gray color over many launderings? Get rid of any that are no longer black (guideline 5) and that are out of style (guideline 1). Do you have a favorite pair of shoes? Can you see the balls of your feet through their soles? Either take them to a cobbler to be repaired or get rid of them (guideline 5).

Many people want to hold on to clothes that are too small or don't fit properly. I know what this is like—my weight has certainly fluctuated over the years. A friend of mine gave me some great advice on this matter a few years ago. She pointed out that every time I saw the smaller clothes I beat myself up over not being able to wear them.

"Opening your closet should be a pleasurable experience," she said. "Ill-fitting clothes are the mean kids on the playground. They tease and bully you into thinking you're not beautiful. You don't need that negative message first thing each morning. Besides, if you get back down to that size, you won't want to wear out-of-style clothes. Surround yourself with clothes that are perfect for you right now."

I completely agree with her sentiment, and that is why I created my second guideline: The item should fit you well and complement your body shape. Stop waiting to fit into your slimmer jeans and buy yourself a sexy new pair.

Many organizers preach that an individual should purge any item in her closet that she hasn't worn in six months. This is a good rule if you live in a single-climate location. However, most of us live in places with four seasons, and it can easily be six months since you last wore a sweater or swimsuit. Instead of using the six-month rule, I like to approach closet purging from a seasonal perspective. If a season ends and you haven't worn a piece of clothing for that season during that time, get rid of it. I also think of a season in a broader sense than calendar months. For instance, I have a beautifully tailored, classic black suit that I wear to funerals. Thankfully, years may pass without my having to wear it. Since I wore the suit to the last funeral I attended, I keep it in my closet. I don't have the time or money to buy a new black suit every time I have to go to a funeral. I think of the suit as being worn during the unfortunate funeral season. As you're going through your clothing, think of the last season when the item was appropriate, and purge the items that you didn't wear in their season.

Wedding dresses are the third rail in my profession. I have received more hate mail from readers disagreeing with my position on what to do with wedding dresses than any other topic. My advice: Sell them; donate them to charity; cut them up and reuse the fabric for baptismal gowns, handkerchiefs, or quilt squares; or redesign them into something you can wear again like Andie Walsh did in the movie *Pretty in Pink*. The dress is just fabric, thread, beads, and buttons. It doesn't hold magical properties. The fate of your marriage is not based on whether you get rid of your wedding dress.

How You Process Information

Your next step is to evaluate your *keep* pile. First, determine whether you have enough room in your closet and dresser for all of the clothes you want to keep. If you don't have enough storage space, you will need to create additional guidelines and sort through your pile again. You cannot keep more clothes than you have space to store. Having more clothes than storage space means that you will always have dirty laundry and you will always have clutter in your wardrobe. Remember the Unclutterer motto: A place for everything, and everything in its place. If you need to reduce the size of your wardrobe further, additional guidelines you might want to consider are the quality of the garment (well-made clothing will last longer) or whether it's easily laundered (this will reduce trips to the dry cleaner).

Once you have everything ready to return to your closet, you have to decide how you will organize your clothes. Contrary to some peoples' beliefs, there is more than one way to organize your closet. To determine what method will work best for you, you need to figure out how you process information: visually, auditorily, or kinesthetically. Deciding what to wear is different for each type of processor. The way you set up your closet now will make it easier to maintain order in the future. Don't know how you process information? Answer the following questions to discover your strengths.

Visual Processors

☐ Do you remember to-do items best if you write them down?

☐ Do you need to visualize yourself wearing something to make a decision about what you want to wear?

☐ Do you take copious notes during meetings and often remember what the page of notes looks like before remembering what the notes say?

☐ Do you need to watch a person when he or she is speaking?

☐ Do you prefer your office to be quiet when you do your work?

☐ Do you prefer seeing numerical information in graphs or charts to better understand the data?

☐ Do you remember phone numbers better if you visualize punching them on a phone's keypad?

Auditory Processors

☐ Do you prefer to listen to books on tape or to read books aloud?

☐ Do you find it's easier to solve a problem at work if you talk it out with coworkers?

☐ In school, did you need only to attend class lectures and listen to the teacher to do well on tests?

☐ Do you remember what people have said to you before you remember what they look like?

☐ Do you like to complete one task before starting a new one?

☐ When you forget how to spell a word, do you sound it out?

☐ At the grocery store, do you repeat your shopping list over and over in your head or quietly aloud?

Kinesthetic/Tactile Processors

☐ When you start a project, do you prefer to begin doing instead of planning?

☐ When you need to take a break from working, do you want to get up and walk around your office?

☐ Can you work effectively in a coffee shop or in an airport waiting room?

☐ Can you remember someone's name better if you shake his or her hand?

☐ Would you like to ride your bike to work, if you don't already?

☐ Do you think more clearly throughout the day if you exercise first thing in the morning?

☐ Are you often aware of the temperature in your office?

☐ When you pick up something as ordinary as a stapler, do you connect it with other memories?

One of these types of information processing will connect with you more than the others. You may have answered yes to questions in all of the categories, but one category should be a better fit than the others. For instance, I am a visual processor with some kinesthetic processing in the mix. Check out the tips in the following paragraphs that correspond to the way you process information, and see the tips on clustering that start on page 33 before you begin organizing the clothes that you're keeping.

If you're a *visual processor:* Have fewer clothes in your closet than your closet can hold. You need space to push your clothes around to get full views of the items you're considering. A hook on the back of your closet door can be beneficial to hang pieces on when coordinating an outfit. You should cluster your clothes by type, situation, or outfit. You may also appreciate having multiple brackets and rods that point outward (manufacturers call these valet rods) instead of or in addition to traditional side-to-

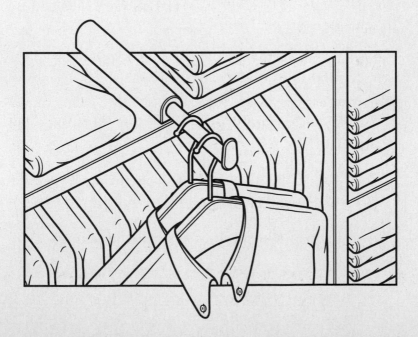

side rods. This way, your clothes will be facing you with a full view instead of a limited side view. Folded and stacked clothes in open cubbies or on shelves might work better for you than dresser drawers. If you use boxes for sweater or shoe storage, be certain to label them or use clear storage boxes so you can see what is inside.

If you're an *auditory processor:* Auditory processors can adapt to most closet organizing systems. Labels are good to put on shelves and containers because when you read the word you will say it to yourself or aloud and better process the information. Different hangers for each cluster of clothing may also prove beneficial to you. Just be sure to enlist a mnemonic or alliteration device in your system, e.g., pink-colored hangers for slacks, brown hangers for blouses, etc. You'll find it easy to decide what to wear as long as your space is organized and clutter free.

If you're a *kinesthetic/tactile processor:* You need space to move while making decisions about what to wear. If you don't have a walk-in closet, keep the space near the door to your closet free of obstructions. Having fewer clothes will also help you make easier decisions, but it will be difficult since you likely have many different purposes for your clothing: office wear, running wear, etc. You probably need to touch your clothes to make a decision about them, so you won't want your clothing rod crammed to its full potential. When you cluster your clothing, consider organizing by purpose, which will help you to know your options for a specific situation. In fact, you may want to group clothing by complete outfits so that you can easily grab and go when you're in a hurry. Since you may like to try on different outfits before choosing the best one to wear, you'll need to make an effort to return the rejected items back to their proper home. And, as I suggested for visual processors, a hook on the back of your closet door or a valet rod is a great idea. Once you select an outfit, hang it on the hook.

Clustering Your Clothes

Clustering is the simple process of hanging your clothes in groups in your closet. There are numerous ways you can cluster your clothes, and you'll have to decide which system works best for you.

- *Type.* Group all similar types of clothing together, pants with pants and dresses with dresses. Stagger the types so that there is a visual distinction between groups of clothing. Moving from left to right, hang suit coats, slacks/pants, short-sleeve shirts, skirts or ties, long-sleeve shirts, and dresses.

- *Color.* You can order your full closet according to color or order individual clusters by color. I organize my closet first by type and then by color within the type. I usually start with blacks and dark blues and work my way through the color spectrum to bright whites.

- *Situation.* If you're someone who has many different purposes for your clothing, organizing by situation might be your best solution. Group together all of your workout clothes, your business professional clothes, your business casual clothes, or whatever kind of clothes you wear.

- *Rotation.* A woman I once worked with wore a different outfit every day of the year. After working with her for multiple years, I discovered that she repeated outfits on the same day each year (she wore the same outfit on December 14, 2005, as she did on December 14, 2006). She pulled an outfit from the left side of her closet, wore it, and then returned it to the right side of her closet. I don't recommend that anyone have so much clothing that he or she can go an entire year without repeating an outfit, but a two- or three-week rotation can be a great idea. Just line your clothes up in the order you wish to wear them.

- *Outfit.* Under this system, you'd probably not use a hanging rod but a series of cubbies. You fold each outfit and put the socks, underwear, and everything you would wear except for shoes in one box. This is a great idea for children who are interested in getting dressed without help, and also for people who work in environments that don't require suits. It takes a while to become accustomed to the system—especially when putting away clean laundry, because you have to make sure each cubby gets all of the pieces of the outfit—but it might be the perfect system for you.

- *Season.* If you don't have much clothing, you may find you can simply organize your clothes by season. Winter, spring, summer, and fall each get their own section of your wardrobe.

When choosing which clustering system to use, be honest with yourself about your level of commitment to maintaining it.

If you won't maintain the system, don't pick it. Remember that you're organizing your closet to help make *your* days less stressful. Now put away the clothes that you have decided to keep.

If you use a dresser or shelving unit for folded clothes, don't forget to include these items in your wardrobe organizing project. When replacing clothes in this furniture, keep space around your clothing so that you can see what folded items are contained inside. The extra space also keeps clothing from wrinkling.

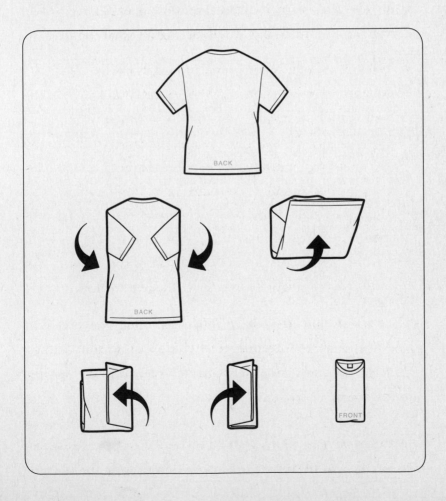

Many people also keep belts, purses, scarves, shoe polishing kits, and other items stored in their bedroom closet. If this is you, don't ignore these pieces as you're organizing your space. Weed out the pieces that you don't need or that are past their prime, and properly store the items that you choose to keep.

I usually leave shoes as the last items to return to the closet. Sort your shoes according to your established guidelines and be sure to store them so that they won't scuff one another. Shoe racks, shoe cubbies, clear shoe boxes, boxes with pictures of the shoes attached to their fronts, and shoe pockets are all great ways to store shoes. If you wear leather shoes, keep some shoe trees on hand to put in your shoes to help retain their shape.

After your *keep* clothes are properly stored, it's time to turn to those other two piles. Sort through your *purge* pile and decide which clothes are of next-to-new quality and which ones are worthy of becoming rags. The clothes that are in decent condition can be donated to charity, sold to a consignment shop, or passed along to friends. The clothing that has seen better days can be bundled up as rags and dropped off at a clothing recycling center or cut up and used as rags in your own home. Some national charities will accept bundled rags and donate them to a recycling center for profit, so call your favorite charity to see if they might be interested in your donation. Try to purge your *purge* pile as quickly as possible so that it doesn't become another source of clutter in your life.

Take action on the clothing that landed in the *extra attention* pile. If a piece of clothing needs to be repaired, do it yourself or take it to a tailor. If you borrowed an item from a friend, set a date to return it. Any shoes that need some love and care should be taken to a cobbler. Don't procrastinate.

In addition to the items that you wear, keep these essential objects in (or close to) to your closet:

- *Small trash can.* Instead of having to traipse across your bedroom to throw away clothing tags, dry cleaning plastic bags, and loose threads, put a trash can in your closet and throw these pieces away conveniently. If your closet is small, like mine, use a large plastic cup.

- *Magnetic strip.* A foot-long piece of magnet affixed to the back of your closet door or the lip of a shelf is a perfect spot to hold stray safety pins, a pair of safety scissors, and a metal basket for a small sewing kit and a stain stick.

- *Hooks.* The back of the closet door is a perfect place for a couple of hooks. Use one to hang up your clothes for the day or to hold your sort-of-dirty pajamas when you're not wearing them.

- *Three bags or boxes.* Drawstring bags or small boxes labeled *Mending, Special Care,* and *Donation* are great to keep in your closet. Put clothes that need to go to the tailor in your *Mending* bag, dirty delicates and/or dry cleaning items in the *Special Care* bag so that they don't get mixed in with your regular laundry, and clothes you wish to donate to charity in the *Donation* bag. Routinely address the contents of these bags so that they don't become overflowing. Your *Mending* and *Donation* bags need to be processed at least once a month, and your *Special Care* bag should be hand washed or dropped off at the dry cleaner when you do the rest of your laundry.

Maintaining Order in Your Closet

The first morning you wake up and experience your organized closet, breathe in the calm and enjoy a couple more minutes of relaxation. You may discover that in a few weeks you will want to do a second round of purging. I typically find there are one or two pieces in my wardrobe that seem to scream, "You should have given me to charity!" You may feel the calling to get rid of even more.

Once a month you will want to take a few minutes to look over your wardrobe and complete any necessary maintenance. Make sure that there aren't any problem areas, that your clothes adhere to your wardrobe guidelines, and that the space is still well organized. If you swap out clothing between seasons, complete a mini closet-organizing project at that time. Even with regular maintenance, you should repeat the whole of this process every year or every other year. Your priorities about your clothing change with time, and reviewing your wardrobe periodically makes sure you are keeping current with your preferences.

Laundry and Caring for Your Wardrobe

While we're talking about clothing, it's only appropriate that we discuss laundry. Just because it's a boring chore doesn't mean you should ignore it.

Out of all of the advice I'm about to give on how to do laundry efficiently, there is one principle that stands out among the others: *The less you own, the less you have to clean.* If you don't have many clothes, then your laundry baskets can't overflow with items. This principle is true for everything in your home (fewer objects to dust, fewer papers to file) and makes a significant impact when you apply it to your wardrobe.

 Tips for keeping laundry under control:

For the person who doesn't mind laundry too much:

- *Decrease the size of your hamper.* It's easy to resist doing laundry until your hamper is full, so use a smaller hamper to keep from getting overwhelmed. Alternatively, most residential washing machines only hold between twelve and eighteen pounds per load (check with your manufacturer for your model's exact weight limit). Get out your scale, put your hamper on the scale, and note the weight. Then fill the hamper with clothes until your scale reads twelve pounds (or whatever your machine's limit) above the weight of the hamper. Mark that clothing line on the inside of your hamper so that you know when you've reached your one-load limit. (Note: Most washing machines will hold more clothing than their weight limit. Just because they can, it doesn't mean they should. Your machine will last longer if you follow the manufacturer's guidelines.)

- *Organize immediately.* If you sort your laundry by color and separate out the delicates and dry cleaning, do this when you take off your clothes.

- *Make it desirable.* The nicer your laundry room, the more time you'll want to spend there. Replace lightbulbs, clear the spiderwebs, and set up a table to fold clothes on. If you don't have a washing machine in your home, keep a piggy bank for quarter collection and carry your detergent in water bottles instead of the hefty container it came in. The easier it is to get to the Laundromat, the more likely you'll be to make a habit of going there.

- *Stay on a routine.* I'll talk about this more in detail in chapter 3.

For the person who hates laundry, see everything listed in the "doesn't mind it too much" section, plus:

- *Get ready for bed at least an hour before you go to bed.* If you're someone who leaves your clothes on the floor instead of in the hamper, it's probably because you're exhausted and climbing into bed in the dark. Get ready for bed when you're still alert and the lights are on to keep you from using your floor as a hamper.

- *Wash-and-wear is the way to go.* Any clothing that requires special attention can clog up your laundry system. If you pay a few extra dollars in the store for wrinkle-free fabrics and wash-and-wear items, you end up saving yourself considerable time (no ironing) and money (no dry cleaning bills) over the long term.

For the person who loathes laundry with the burning passion of a thousand suns, see everything listed in the "doesn't mind it too much" and "hates it" sections, plus:

- *Avoid colors that bleed.* If you don't have darks that bleed onto lights, then you can throw everything into the same load. Reds, oranges, blacks, purples, and navy blues are often bleeders, so avoid them for convenience.

- *Buy in bulk.* Stop wasting time matching socks. Buy multiple pairs of the same kind of sports and dress socks. I buy six pairs of identical white sports socks and five pairs of identical dark dress socks. When they start to wear out, I turn all of them into rags and replace them at the same time. In my house, we call it the Sock Purge, and it takes place about every six to eight months.

With your closet in order and your laundry done, it's time for you to head to work. As the week progresses, you'll work through other areas in your home that still need attention. But right now, stay on target and get ready to tackle the rest of your "firsts."

Monday at Work:
Your Office

In the same way that you first see your closet when you wake up in the morning, your desk is the first thing you see when you walk into your office. It's the focal point of every office, and when it's organized and free of clutter it becomes your canvas for efficient and productive work.

Your desk is also the first thing others see when they walk into your office. Earlier, I talked about how people see the way you're dressed and make assumptions—both accurate and inaccurate—about who you are. Visual clues provide people with information about how to interact with you. You use these cues, too. When you're sitting in a restaurant, if someone walks up to your table wearing an apron and holding a pen and a pad of paper, your assumption is that it's okay to hand this stranger your credit card to pay for your meal. The visual cues work with the knowledge you have about how restaurants operate, and you are probably correct in thinking that the person is a waiter or waitress.

In the same way, the state of your office sends messages about what kind of a worker you are. Having a chronically disorganized office screams, "I am an ineffective worker!" This may not seem like such a big deal, but these perceptions can end up having a negative impact on your career.

Perceptions

Like it or not, your coworkers and clients make assumptions about you based on what they see. There are two sets of cues that they read about you: superficial and personal cues. Superficial cues come from objects like your office furniture (I have a large wooden desk, I'm important!), framed diplomas (I survived college!), and the giant mess on your desk (I don't know how to file or take dishes to the kitchen!). Personal cues come from objects like photographs (I have a family and a dog!), coffee mugs (I went to a conference in Toledo!), and knickknacks from other aspects of your life (This concert ticket is proof that I don't live in this cubicle!).

If a manager, coworker, or client sees work from many months ago still gracing the top of your desk, he will assume that you've been goofing off or lack basic organizing skills. If your boss sees that your office is cluttered with dozens of ski lift tickets from your past vacations, she's going to assume that you would rather be skiing than working. And, be honest, these assumptions are probably spot-on—you would rather be in Colorado skiing than sitting at your desk. This means that not only is your messy office keeping you from working efficiently, but it also may be costing you a promotion, client, or raise because of the negative messages it's relaying.

Professional business adviser Penelope Trunk explains, "A messy desk undermines your career in subtle ways. If you are the owner of the company, you give the impression that you cannot handle your position and the company is in trouble. If you are in middle management, when someone is giving away a plumb [*sic*] assignment, she does not think of you because you give the impression that it will go into a pile and never come out. Even if you get every project done well, the perception will be that you don't."[3]

I'm not suggesting that your office has to be a minimalist, sanitized, or soulless environment. A well-decorated and organized office can communicate positive opinions about your work and personality. One or two personal items can create talking points for people who come into your office. Having a plant on your desk can even lead people to think that you're a team player.[4]

Hang your framed diploma on a wall (boring, yes, but good for people who make superficial assumptions), change the wallpaper on your computer's desktop to an image related to your favorite hobby or travel destination (instead of filling your office with nonwork items), put a healthy plant on the top of your filing cabinet (show that you're a team player), set a picture of your loved ones on your desk (this is for those people who make personal assumptions, and to bring you a bit of joy), and get rid of all other personal items. In a competitive marketplace, a clean, organized, well-decorated office might be the key to keeping your job, earning a raise, retaining a client, or being promoted, irrespective of the quality of work you actually do.

Organizing and Maintaining Your Desk

Whipping your office into shape is easy if you separate it into two activities. The first activity is getting your physical space in order and the second activity is getting your paper mess under control. I'll help you with your physical space now, and tomorrow I'll give you advice on taming your paper piles. So, for the time being, if you have paper stacks on your work surfaces, you'll want to pile these in another room on a conference table or on an empty desk.

Along with your stacks of paper, move the rest of your equipment off of your desk. When you can only see your desk, take this opportunity to scrub away the dirt, dust, and grime.

If you work in a cubicle, you don't have much say about the placement of your desk. People with desks that aren't attached to the wall, however, can decide if the desk is in the best location. There is a great deal of research available about how to arrange furniture and you may wish to check it out, but there are three major things that you'll want to consider now:

1. *Entrance/exit path.* In case of an emergency, you want to be able to leave your desk quickly and safely.

2. *Lighting.* You want to be able to see your work throughout the day, but you don't want to fight with glare or depth-of-vision issues.

3. *Ergonomics.* Avoid a poor setup that can result in back, arm, hand, and neck problems.

Once your desk has a set location, decide where to put your office equipment. Grab your chair and your keyboard and find the spot on the desk that is the most conducive to comfortable work. With these pieces in place, you can set up the remainder of your desk. The extreme minimalist can get away with nothing but a laptop, a scanner, and their power cords. I'm not a minimalist and prefer to have more accessories within my reach while I work.

If you have to lean, stretch, or, worse yet, stand up to get a piece of equipment you regularly use, you're going to waste time when you work. That means your computer, monitor, keyboard, mouse, backup hard drive, printer, scanner, and telephone probably need to be within the reach of your extended arms when you're sitting in your desk chair. To increase productivity, I also recommend using a second monitor (the additional screen space is reported to improve productivity by an average of 42 percent because you don't have to open multiple programs and flip between them[5]), which means another piece of equipment to add to the mix. Keep in mind, however, that *the only items on the top of your desk should be those things you reach for on a regular basis.* If you use something less than twice a day, consider storing that item in a desk drawer or cupboard. If you have a phone on your desk, be sure to set it to the right of your computer if you answer the phone with your right hand and to the left of your computer if you prefer your left.

The ways in which you can reduce clutter and organize your desk are endless. Just remember that your desk is there to facilitate work and should be organized accordingly. Put items where you use them, and have your trash can and shredder accessible from all locations in your space. Group items with like items, and place objects you share with other employees in a spot they can get to quickly.

As you're setting up the equipment on your desk, ask yourself if you have the best equipment for your work. The right tools can make a difference in the quality of your work and the speed with which you do it. Your computer, printer, phone, stapler, and desk chair support you (literally and figuratively) as you perform your job. In fact, a good rule of thumb is if a piece of equipment isn't helping you, then it's time to get rid of it.

What equipment do you have? Is any of it broken? Is there any equipment in your office that you don't use? Are you storing someone else's equipment in your office? Also ask the questions for your things from the Foundations chapter (page 9).

Get rid of any equipment that you don't use and put in a request with your purchasing department to replace any equipment that is broken. If you're storing equipment for someone else, move it out. Your office should be free of any and all equipment that doesn't advance or support your work.

The next step is to evaluate the equipment that you use and decide whether it's the best product for the job. Does it need to be cleaned? Does it do what it's supposed to do? Is it hindering your performance more than it's helping?

Submit a service request for any equipment that needs to be cleaned or upgraded, and replace any equipment that is preventing you from doing your job. Even if your employer doesn't get you what you need immediately, they can budget for it in the future. You don't need to shell out thousands of dollars to buy the most expensive machines—especially if you won't ever take advantage of all of their features—but you should at least have functioning equipment in your office that fulfills its purpose. The right tools are essential to your performance.

If you decide to get rid of any electronic equipment, either recycle it with the manufacturer or a local electronics store (like

Best Buy), or donate it to a charity that accepts these types of donations. Be sure to erase all hard drives before you send them away for disposal or recycling. You can find hard drive erasing programs online. I recommend Disk Utility for a Mac and Darik's Boot and Nuke for a PC. Just be sure to save everything you want beforehand, because once you erase your hard drive, it's gone.

When you've decided what equipment can stay and you're ready to hook it back up, spend some time making sure that your cables don't become a bird's nest. Label both ends of all of your power cords and computer cables. Labeling makes things simple when you need to unplug something on the power strip and you're in that awkward position crouched beneath your desk. Print sticky labels with a label maker, or write on masking tape with a permanent marker. Once your cables are labeled, consider using one of the following products to keep your cables from being cluttered:

String. Sometimes the simplest of products can do amazing work. Wrap string around coiled cords, tie a bow, and call it a day. If you want to get creative, use different-colored yarn for each cord and put a corresponding color-coordinated dot on the plug for easy identification.

Velcro Ties. Exactly like string, but with Velcro.

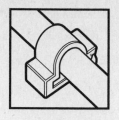

Cable Clips. Get rid of dangling cables by attaching cable clips to your desk legs or wall and feeding your cords through the clips.

Turtles. Flip up the shell, eliminate cable slack by winding it around the Turtle, and then flip the shell over the cable.

Nylon Cable Ties. Well-insulated cords and cables can be zipped together with cable ties. Just be careful not to slice into the cords when you trim the tail.

Retractable Cords. Standard computer cables can sometimes be replaced with retractable versions, especially when both connectors are the same, like USB to USB.

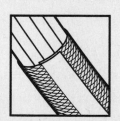

Cable Bundler Tubes. These tubes are usually plastic and have a slit to push multiple cords into the tube. The diameter of the tube determines how many cords you can run through them. These are great to use when you have cords that need to run along a section of visible space, like baseboards or the back of your desk.

While I'm talking about office equipment, I also want to mention that you should always take the time to read equipment manuals. The same is true for software. Money and time are needlessly wasted when you don't know your equipment and software well. And since some software is extremely complicated and rich with features, don't be afraid to take a class that explains all of them. A few hours in a class will quickly be recouped when you learn how to navigate through a program at lightning speed.

Organizing the Rest of Your Office

Beyond the equipment on your desk, take the time to organize books, binders, and materials that you need to do your job. Group items by purpose (office supplies in one drawer, binders for project B all on the same shelf, etc.), and label shelves and materials so that a coworker can easily find items when you're pressed for time or absent from work.

Establish an inbox for physical items (like postal mail and things you need to sign) so your manager and coworkers know where they can leave you papers and you will find them. It also helps to keep your desk clear so that you have space to work on other things. When you leave work for the day, your inbox should be empty—no exceptions. Assignments can't slip through the cracks when you are aware of everything you need to do. Process materials in this box a few times a day and take action on each item the first time you touch it. These new habits will help you to better organize your time as well as your office. As a result, you'll be a more efficient, productive, and organized worker.

Monday Evening: Your Reception Station

After a long day of work and running errands, returning home feels incredible. Home is a place for retreat and relaxation. Home is where you connect with family and friends. Home is where you nurture and care for yourself so that you can face all the things life throws in your direction.

When you arrive home, if the first area you see is disorganized and full of clutter, then you become anxious about the mess. You can't recharge and rejuvenate at home if you're overwhelmed by stuff. For the same reasons you first organized your closet and then your desk, organizing the entryway to your home is your final Monday project.

The first place you see when you come home should be welcoming, calm, and free of clutter. Regardless of whether your entryway is located in your foyer, living room, mudroom, or kitchen, it's the next area you need to unclutter and organize.

Creating a Reception Station

Start this process by laying a blanket on the floor of another room and piling onto it all the stuff from your entryway. Once this area is completely empty, you should clean the floor, walls, and any pieces of furniture that exist here. Wipe down shelves, baseboards, and light fixtures. Get this area sparkling clean.

Next, make a plan for the future of this space. Think of this area as the Reception Station for your home and your launchpad to the outside world. You want the area to be inviting and relaxing, but you also want it to store all the things you need to put away when you come home and have available to you when you leave. If you live alone, you'll only have to think about your needs for this space. If you have a roommate, spouse, and/or children, you'll want to include them into the planning of your new Reception Station.

Unless you live in the tropics, you'll want a designated section for hanging up jackets and coats. You'll need a place to sit to remove muddy and wet shoes, and another area to store this messy footwear. You'll want storage for your hats, gloves, and scarves during cooler months. You'll need an area to sort through the day's mail, a trash can, a small shredder (see the box on the following page), a place to put coins, and an inbox. If you have children of school age, you'll need space for their book bags and extracurricular supplies. If you carry a backpack, purse, or briefcase, you'll want a designated space for it to live. Your car and house keys should also have a home. Finally, don't forget your cell phone and any electronic devices that can be charged in this space.

Think of all of the items you waste time trying to find when you need to leave your home, and create a space for these items so that you no longer misplace them. Install hooks, a bench, lockers, or whatever it is you need to make this space functional. If you have a mudroom, you can probably get away with using utilitarian items and not have to worry so much about decoration. If the main entrance to your home is its foyer, you can hide a shredder and a recycling bin in a nice cupboard and use the top of the piece for decorative storage boxes for gloves and scarves. Find pieces that meet your needs and decor.

Why do I love shredders so much? Because they keep your personal information out of the hands of identity thieves. A single preapproved credit card offer can be the ticket to the good life for someone who finds it after you've thrown it away. To protect yourself, shred all trash that leaves your home that bears your name, address, and even more valuable personal information. The few seconds it takes to shred these items is nothing compared to the months it takes to fight identity theft claims.

Once your space has been outfitted with a storage system, it's time to sort through the stuff that was previously in this space. Similar to how you cleaned out your wardrobe, get rid of anything that isn't being used. Donate items to charity or toss them in the recycling bin or trash if that is more appropriate. Return things to their appropriate spots in other rooms. Finally, place everything you've chosen to keep into the new storage system you've created in your Reception Station.

Since you've already had a full day, consider making a game of this process to keep up your momentum. Race your spouse through equal piles, and the loser has to take the other out for a celebratory dinner. Give yourself two points for every item you donate to charity or recycle, but subtract one point for every item you keep. If you come out with a positive score, reward yourself. Sorting and purging isn't exciting, but you will appreciate your work once it's behind you.

Coming Home

If you're like me, coming home is a great relief at the end of the day. It represents shutting out the world beyond my door and relaxing with my family. Dumping your things onto the floor or strewing them around your living room, however, isn't going to help you the next time you need to leave your house, and it certainly won't help you relax. As important as it was to create the Reception Station, it's equally important to take advantage of it every time you come home.

Start by setting your briefcase, purse, and/or backpack in its newly designated space. Remove your coat, gloves, and scarf if it's during the cold season. Hang and store these items so they can dry and be ready the next time you brave the elements. If you need to remove your shoes, take a seat and do this now. Set your shoes on a drying rack if they're wet. Wipe down the floor with an old towel or rag if you brought sand, snow, or rain in with you from the outdoors. I keep a stack of four or five rags folded inside a bin in my Reception Station for just this purpose.

Immediately sort through your mail and shred any junk mail with personal information on it, like credit card applications. Toss all other junk mail into the recycling bin. Distribute mail for other people in your house into designated cubbies or hanging pockets so they know exactly where to find it. At this point, open up your mail and write future actions that need to be taken and notes to yourself on their envelopes ("pay bill," "send thank-you card," etc.). Empty your pockets or your purse of all clutter. Put coins into a piggy bank or coin sorter. Throw away useless receipts for cash purchases for consumable goods you've already consumed (coffee receipts, for instance). Heat-imprinted receipts usually can't be recycled, so it's okay if you throw these directly into the trash. If you keep a ledger of your cash expenditures, you'll want to note these purchases before you get rid of the receipt. All other receipts for debit card, check, and credit card purchases should be retained in an envelope and reconciled with your bank statement at the end of the month. (After reconciling, you'll want to shred all receipts except those for items you may return, for large purchases that have warranties, and for tax-deductible items. We'll talk about how to retain these receipts in the next chapter.) All other pocket trash should be thrown away before you take a single step further into your home. Put away your keys and charge your cell phone and any electronic devices you typically carry with you throughout the day.

Any materials you'll need out of your briefcase, backpack, or purse during the evening should be retrieved now. Have your children pull any papers that need to be signed out of their backpacks immediately when they come home. Lunch sacks also need to come out and not linger in bags. If you pulled your briefcase, backpack, or purse out to retrieve items, don't forget to put it back in its place.

Pick up your mail and any other items that need further processing and enter your house. Your Reception Station is now set and ready to go in the morning.

Maintaining Your Reception Station

At least once a month, set aside a fifteen-minute block of time to go through your Reception Station and clear any clutter that may have accidentally taken up residence in this space. Rearrange it a bit at the end of the summer and winter seasons to make sure it will suit all of your needs for the next six months. Also, don't forget to empty the shredder, recycling bin, and trash can on a weekly basis (or more often, if needed).

An organized Reception Station means never losing your keys or bringing clutter into your home. During my days as a clutterbug, it never occurred to me that I could get out the door without hunting for something (or forgetting something). Now I know that if there is ever an emergency, I can get out the door safely in just a few seconds.

chapter 3

Tuesday

Researchers in Britain[6] have found the exact time when people feel the most stress during the week: Tuesday at 11:45 AM.

This is when the reality of all you need to accomplish for the week sets in and you realize you'd better get your bum in gear. Tuesday is the true workhorse of the week. It's the day when you push up your sleeves and get down to business.

Today's schedule includes uncluttering the bathroom, your papers, and your files and streamlining your household chores. These are the three areas of your life that require the most attention to make them work for you, and following my proposed changes will significantly improve the way you live.

Tuesday Morning: Your Bathroom

For most of us, the only time we think about our bathrooms is when we're in them or if something in them has stopped working. They serve a specific purpose, are in a fixed location, and are only used when necessary.

As a result, things tend to come into bathrooms and never leave: shampoo, lotion, brushes, decorative soaps, pain relievers, cough medicines. If your bathroom is filled with clutter, I wouldn't be surprised. Welcome to the club!

Bathrooms are an integral aspect of the morning routine, and clutter in this space can easily affect your outlook on your day. With an organized, clutter-free bathroom, you won't have to hunt for a hairbrush or get caught in the shower without any soap—or with more soap than you could possibly need.

Define Your Bathroom's Purposes

This may sound like a ridiculous task, but I want you to identify and create a list of all of the purposes for your bathroom. Some options you may consider are: showering, relaxing in the bath, putting on makeup, using the toilet, teeth brushing, shaving, painting your nails, nail trimming, dirty clothes collection (is there a hamper in your space?), weighing yourself, medication storage, linen storage, cleaning supply storage, and information gathering (is there a radio or television in your space?). For such a banal and small space, I'm always surprised by how many purposes it serves. Knowing how you use this space can go a long way toward helping you organize it.

Organizing Your Bathroom by Zones

Pull everything except for the permanent structures out of your bathroom—soap, shampoo, curling irons, razors, towels, etc. As you are extracting everything from the space, create piles according to the purposes you just listed. Put together things that are used together—all your shaving supplies in one pile, all your medicines in another.

Sort through these groups one at a time. For now, put all duplicates, expired products, and things you don't use into a laundry basket. Weed out all the clutter from your piles so that only the things you need and use remain. I find it useful to ask myself, "Would I buy this again?" If the answer is no, then I move the item out of its pile and put it into the laundry basket.

Now that your piles are free of clutter, you're ready to create zones in your bathroom to fully utilize your space and make your morning routine faster and easier. Zones are the areas where you store the items that fulfill the purposes of the room. Just like your piles, you'll have a teeth-brushing zone, a hair-washing zone, etc. As you're creating these zones, set them up by convenience—locate things based on where you use them and the order in which you access them. If you're putting things into drawers, use dishwasher-safe dividers to group your products for each purpose. I like to use small plastic boxes that I can pull out and rest on the counter when I'm using the products, and then put the box back into the drawer when I'm finished.

If more than one person uses the space, you might want to establish your zones by "mine" and "not mine." Designate baskets, drawers, and shelves for users so that one person's things don't invade another person's space. Decide what is appropriate to leave on the counter and what needs to be put away so that no one has to deal with another person's mess.

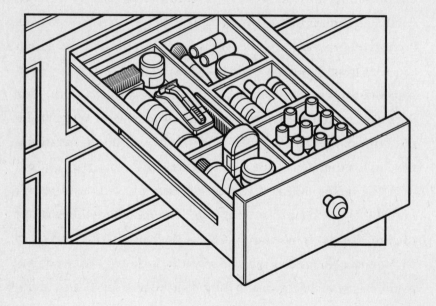

If you choose to purchase or repurpose bins, baskets, or boxes for storage in your bathroom, remember two simple words: *water resistant*. Plastic, metal, bamboo, and fabrics will last longer in your bathroom than cardboard or other paper products. If you choose to use metal storage products, use naturally rustproof metal products (like aluminum) or treat the metal with an antirust spray.

Cabinet Clearing

When you're returning items to your bathroom cabinet, re-member that you should *not* store medicine in it. Highly humid and hot environments (like your bathroom when you take a shower) can degrade and damage your medicines. Susan Mar-tin, a pharmaceutical chemist, explained it to me as being simi-lar to holding a piece of hard candy in the palm of your hand; it will get gummy after a few minutes. The moisture from your hand (your sweat) chemically changes the candy. Unlike with a candy getting gummy in the palm of your hand, it can be diffi-cult to know when a chemical change has taken place in your medicine, which could end up as a poison in your body. To be safe, you should store your medicines in a cool, dry, dark loca-tion unless specifically instructed otherwise on the drug's label.

Additionally, most medicine cabinets in bathrooms don't have locks on them. To keep your medications safe and out of little hands or visitors' pockets, all prescription and over-the-counter drugs should be locked in a chest. The medicine cabinet in your bathroom should only be used for less danger-ous items, like hairbrushes, deodorant, and extra rolls of toilet paper.

Also, when you're getting rid of the clutter that you put into the laundry basket, do *not* flush any expired medications or vitamins down your toilet or sink. It's best to take them to pharmacies, city or county hazardous waste facilities, and/or hospitals that commonly accept old prescriptions for proper disposal.

Buy the Small Size

I was thirty-four years old when I learned that lotion had an expiration date. If you have never learned this lesson firsthand, take my word for it. Expired lotion feels like a slimy mixture of sour milk, rotten eggs, and day-old hamburger grease on your skin.

The ingredients in lotion, shampoo, conditioner, sunscreen, hair styling products, facial cleansers, and liquid soap can deteriorate over time and cause the product to go bad. They separate, putrefy, and fail to accomplish their reported claims. The plastic containers they're stored in also start to break down, and the chemicals from the plastic interact with the contents inside. As you're sorting through the products that you put into the laundry basket, you'll want to permanently dispose of any product past its expiration date.

Products typically stored in glass, like nail polish and cologne, run almost no risk of interacting with their containers. However, nail polish can become goopy or dried out if its lid is improperly secured, and cologne can lose its strength if it's not stored in a cool, dark location. Get rid of either product if it's not doing its job.

If you're unsure of a product's expiration date, pick up the phone and give its manufacturer's customer service line a call. They'll likely ask you for the code printed on the bottle (usually on its bottom), so be sure to have the product nearby. You may be surprised to learn that many of the items you've been using are better suited for the trash and/or recycling. An alternative to multiple phone calls is to let your nose be your guide. Smell the product before using it—if the product smells different than it did when it was new, it's best not to use it.

Other products you have in your bathroom may still be good, but you may have grown bored with them. I often like a product for a while but want to try something different. My friends are the same way, and so we'll swap bottles of liquids that are mostly used but we know we're never going to finish. You may be okay with ginger-scented shampoo in the summer, but in the fall you might want a cedar-scented product.

If you're like me and have trouble using products before their expiration dates, take the following plan of action:

1. Purge all expired products from your bathroom.

2. Commit to using up what you have before buying any newer products. One in, one out.

3. Have a swap event with your friends if you're looking for an alternative to using up the products yourself.

4. Only buy small bottles of products in the future so that you'll use it all up before it goes bad or you become bored with it.

There is a caveat to this process: If you have a large family and you all use the same bath products, buying small might be a ridiculous suggestion for you. It is more economical to buy the larger size, but only if you're using the entire product. Stay true to the "one in, one out" rule and you'll be fine.

How Much Is Enough?

During its second season in 1967, the television show *Star Trek* aired an episode called "The Trouble with Tribbles." In this episode, a member of the crew of the Starship *Enterprise* is given a cuddly, furry tribble as a pet. Unfortunately for the crew, the tribble reproduces at an alarming rate and thousands of tribbles end up eating all of the grain on the ship. The crew runs the risk of dying of starvation out in deep space since their food supply has been so greatly depleted. I won't give away details about the ending of the episode, but since the show went on to run for another season and a half, you can probably guess that they found a way out of the furry situation.

I mention this episode of *Star Trek* because I remember thinking about it the first time I cleared the clutter from my linen storage. I was convinced that my bath towels and washcloths had multiplied. I remembered buying one of the towels before I started college, but I had no memory of how I acquired the dozens more in the years since. It was as if they had spontaneously reproduced while the doors to the linen closet were shut.

To determine how many towels and washcloths you need, use this simple math equation:

(House residents + Guest bedrooms) × 2 = Sets of bath towels and washcloths

The logic behind the equation is that you have one bath towel and washcloth in use and another set in the linen closet ready to go. Since houseguests only need towels while they're staying with you, they don't need extras in reserve. Most guest rooms can accommodate two people, so multiplying the number of guest rooms by two usually provides for a towel per guest. (I'm using the term *guest room* in a general sense; in our house the guest room is an apple-green pullout couch in the middle of the living room.) If you have four people living in your home and zero guest rooms, then you should have eight bath towels and eight washcloths: $(4 + 0) \times 2 = 8$. If you have three people living in your home and two guest rooms, then you should have ten towels and ten washcloths: $(3 + 2) \times 2 = 10$.

This equation might not work for everyone, but most people find it to be a good starting point. If you're a whiz at laundry, you might be able to get by on one set of towels per person. If you're particular about having a new washcloth every day, you might need more washcloths in your collection. If your towels are falling on your head every time you open your linen closet, it's time to trim your collection.

One nice thing about getting rid of towels and washcloths is that animal shelters worldwide are more than eager to take used linens off your hands. They are used to provide soft spaces for animals to rest, to dry off recently bathed animals, and to clean up messes. In addition to towels and washcloths, most shelters also take old sheets and tablecloths. Give your favorite animal shelter a call before you make your donation to make sure that they have a need for your unwanted items, and wash the items you plan to donate.

In addition to towels and washcloths, it can be beneficial to set up guidelines for all of the products in your bathroom.

For example, you probably don't need seven hairbrushes. You might, however, regularly use a comb, a round brush, and a flat brush. If this is the case, get rid of the brushes you don't use and only buy new brushes when your current ones need to be replaced.

Toilet paper is another tricky item. It's easy to stock up whenever you come across a good deal. In my home, the guideline is that we never buy more toilet paper than we can store in the designated toilet paper storage area. This storage area can accommodate twenty-four rolls of toilet paper, so we never buy more than twenty-four rolls at a time—no matter how wonderful the discount.

Taking Care of Guests

Are you one of those people who feel compelled to smuggle the little bottles of shampoo, conditioner, and lotion into your luggage every time you leave a hotel? I am. They're small! They're cute! They're free!

Instead of stuffing them into the dark recesses of your linen closet, group them together and make them available to houseguests. I keep a metal box on the counter in my bathroom that says "For all our guests." In the box are samples of products that come in the mail, free toothbrushes I got from the dentist, travel-size products I took with me on vacation and didn't finish using, a few disposable razors, and all of the tiny bottles of shampoo, conditioner, and lotion I've taken from my hotel rooms. I use a box because it matches my home's decor, but you can use a basket, tray, or whatever works best in your space.

The guest box ends up serving many purposes. First, it acts as a storage location for the random things that can accumulate in a bathroom. Second, my guests think I'm considerate for having thought of them. Third, when friends come to stay overnight, someone inevitably forgets to bring a toothbrush or other random item and the guest box keeps him or her from wasting time running to the store. Fourth, since the box says "For all our guests," I've had plumbers, painters, friends, and family members take things they need from the box. The items end up being used by people who want and need them instead of cluttering up the bathroom. I also like to think that it keeps guests from inspecting our bathroom cabinet.

When you don't have to spend your early mornings scrambling to find what you need to get ready, your entire morning ritual is calm, simple, and pleasant. You don't rush, and you certainly don't stress out about hunting down your brush or your razor. A serene morning gives you a clear mind to get started on whatever the day may bring.

Tuesday at Work:
Fixing Your Files

There are two reasons, and only two reasons, to retain papers and files:

1. To Cover Your Ass (CYA): These are the papers you keep because you might be in a bind, lose your job, get sued, lose money, or go to jail if you don't retain them.

2. To Extend Your Knowledge and the Knowledge of Others (Extended Knowledge): These are the papers you keep because they provide you with information you wish you had stored in your brain, but you don't. They're also kept because eventually someone else will need access to your knowledge when you're not around.

There are no other reasons to hold on to papers in your office. You may decide you *want* to hold on to papers for other reasons (you might have a sentimental attachment to a note that you chose not to purge during your "Sentimental Journey" project), but you don't *need* to keep them. Papers that aren't CYA or Extended Knowledge aren't going to earn you a promotion, land you a pay raise, or make you a more productive worker. Any other piece of paper is clutter and doesn't belong in your office even if you have room for it. In fact, having an outdated phone directory on your desk could confuse you, waste time, and create an uncomfortable situation when you leave a message on the wrong person's voice mail.

Actual examples of CYA papers are notarized legal documents, your Social Security card, and the document your boss told you to protect with your life. Extended Knowledge papers are manuals, organizational charts, research, and materials that can be important to the function of your job and institutional history.

You'll come to know these two types of papers as the backbone of your Personal Data Collection (PDC). Your PDC will operate much like a collection in a library or research institution, with processes in place to handle evaluation, categorization, and access to information. (Note: Not all of the information in your PDC will be paper. Digital, multimedia, and three-dimensional objects will likely be included and may even make up the majority of items. I use the word *paper* throughout this section, but I'm referring to all of this data.)

Stop Stacking Papers

If the top of your desk resembles a topographical map, you're likely to defend your piles by explaining to me that you "know where everything is located." I have no doubt that you know where specific papers are. I used to be a stacker, and I always seemed to find what I needed. But finding what you need isn't the only reason you keep papers.

Having organized papers and files not only increases your productivity, it also makes it easier for coworkers to access your data when you're out of the office. Additionally, it indicates to others that you can handle your workload and provide quality service. A PDC allows you to be a more productive and creative worker (see page 72) and feel comfortable in your office. Most important, once you have a good filing system in place, maintaining it will come naturally.

Qualities of a Good Filing System

If you were to create a filing system, how would you be able to tell if you created a good system or not? Beyond the obvious— i.e., your papers are no longer on the floor—how would you know that you had achieved success?

You have achieved success when your filing system has these seven qualities:

1. You're able to search for and find information quickly.

2. Information is organized by categories.

3. The system makes sense to people who don't regularly use it.

4. The system is maintained and is easy to maintain.

5. The system is able to accept new entries easily.

6. Information is categorized consistently.

7. The system identifies broader relationships about the information in the PDC.

Creating a filing system that follows these seven rules is important because the information you keep is valuable, and you want to get the most out of it. While it's obvious that if you put something into a system you want to be able to find it again (quality 1) and no one wants to have to rearrange his entire filing cabinet every time he has a new contract to file (quality 5), the other qualities need a little more explanation.

Quality 2, the categorization quality, is the physical structure for your filing system. Your data should be grouped by units that reflect the work you do. If you have clients, then your system will probably be client based. If you create cogs and widgets, then your system might be product based. Later in the chapter, I'll give you specific advice on how to determine these categories for your work.

Quality 3, the approachability quality, states that your system has to easily make sense to other people. If you go on vacation, a coworker should be able to come to your filing cabinet or computer and find what she needs, and she shouldn't need to use an index or a guidebook to your files. In offices where high security is a must, the information doesn't need to be obvious to a burglar, but it should at least make sense to your colleagues who work within your regular security system.

Quality 4, the maintenance quality, is the basis for most of the ideas in this book. If a system is easy to maintain, it will be maintained. If you don't know how to put information into the system, you're just going to keep stacking.

Quality 6 means that you use the same naming system throughout your filing system. For example, in a *Bedrock* city category, you might have separate client folders for "Flintstone, Fred," "Flintstone, Wilma," "Rubble, Barney," and "Rubble, Betty," with all client folders labeled and alphabetized by last name first, and then first name. Establish a consistent naming pattern and stick to it.

Quality 7, the relational quality, is the most difficult quality to achieve but the most beneficial if you attain it. Without the other six qualities, you will have trouble finding relationships among the information in your collection. The more relationships you can establish and connections you can make, the more helpful your files will be to you and the more creative you will be. I associate it with the old Reese's Peanut Butter Cup commercials where two people run into each other, one carrying a jar of peanut butter and the other a chocolate candy bar. Both the chocolate bar and peanut butter are valuable separately, but when they are accidentally combined they create a third, improved snack. A well-designed filing system allows you to see separate files and identify new connections with that information. Your brain does this naturally, and your filing system should operate in a similar way so that it becomes an extension of your knowledge. You'll work better and be more creative because relationships among points of data will be easier to establish.

A digital filing system best exemplifies quality 7 because it allows you to link one document (or image or whatever you are storing) to many locations. Not only can you create relationships, but you can also identify patterns and perform searches based on individual data points. You can search for and retrieve all files on your computer that contain the word *crayon*. If *crayon* appears on a sign in an image, a good system will even retrieve that image in its results (programs like Evernote do this well). Or, if this is a search you've completed numerous times already, you may choose to create a permanent file in your system that has links to all of your *crayon* documents.

Case Study

While doing research for this chapter, a number of business-people were gracious and let me come into their offices and inspect their files. I didn't care much about the contents of their files, but rather I was interested in how data made it into their company's Data Collection. How did they decide what stayed? How did they organize what they kept? How did they train employees to use the system?

A law firm I studied had the most creative filing structure of the businesses I observed. The firm's clients are dispersed across the United States, and the firm files its papers according to geography. West Coast legal documents can be found on the west side of the file storage room and East Coast files are on the east side. The files are categorized by state and then subcatego-rized by the airport codes within that state. If a lawyer needs to fly into Los Angeles to meet with a client, then the lawyer will find the file under LAX. The firm's filing system is structured to reflect the way the lawyers use the information.

A system like the one at the law firm would be useless to me since location has nothing to do with the work I do, but it works splendidly for the lawyers who use it. And the system the firm uses has its roots in the seven qualities of a good filing system. Information can be retrieved quickly, data is categorized by geographical location, I was able to retrieve data from the system after hearing a brief explanation, the system is maintained, adding files is simple, the information is consistently named, and the lawyers can instantly make connections between client issues just by looking at one airport grouping of files. The firm's files clearly illustrate how a one-size-fits-all system doesn't work for everyone and that understanding how to build a system allows you to create your perfect solution every time.

Structuring Your Filing System

We've already discussed that a PDC should be comprised of CYA and Extended Knowledge documents. To achieve the status of a "good filing system" and its seven qualities, however, you need to make a plan before diving into sorting and scanning. If you plan out your system first, it will make the hands-on portion of this activity simpler, faster, and therefore more productive. Design your best system now and reap its benefits later.

The first stage in planning your filing system is to conduct an initial inventory. What do you have? Start by looking at the big picture:

☐ Do you have papers that can be digitally scanned?

☐ Do you have papers that will need to be housed in a filing cabinet?

☐ Do you have notebooks or manuals that will require bookshelf space?

☐ Is there artwork or other mixed media that will need tubes or hooks or consoles to protect and store the objects?

☐ Are your papers letter or legal size?

☐ Do you have personal papers mixed in with professional papers?

☐ Do you have papers that should be in archives?

☐ Do you have papers that should be in working files?

☐ Do you have multiple copies of a document but in different versions?

Archives are complete units that won't change, and working files are units used on an ongoing basis that do change. You might find it beneficial to keep these two categories separated in different drawers or cabinets.

Once you've addressed the big-picture questions, focus on specific content. You'll have to touch your papers and files at this point, but don't think about purging or sorting. Just poke around your documents and identify what you have. I like to think of this stage as sizing up the situation. Keep a sheet of paper and a pen nearby to take notes on what you discover. Your notes should be general and reflect the content of your documents (memos from the HR department, contracts with X vendor, annual reports), but they need to include specific categories so that you'll remember what you're referencing ("memos" is likely too vague for your system). As you're taking notes, you'll notice patterns emerge, and those patterns will be important in the next couple of stages.

The second stage in planning your filing system is to set guidelines for purging. What rules should define what will stay and what will go? You already know part of the answer to this question—CYA and Extended Knowledge papers will stay—but you'll need to establish the parameters for making these decisions. The parameters I use are:

- If I get rid of this, will I be in a serious bind, lose my job, get sued, lose an irreplaceable amount of money, or go to jail?

- Do I want to have this knowledge at my fingertips and will I have a difficult time getting my hands on this information later if I don't retain this document?

- Will keeping this document make it easier for someone else if I am unavailable?

After getting the rules for deciding what stays and what goes, the third stage in your planning process will be to establish the structure of your system. Classifying and categorizing information is nothing more than identifying patterns you want to highlight in your PDC. What makes this part of this process difficult is that there are limitless patterns in your data that you can highlight.

The patterns you decide to use should reflect the content and purpose of your documents. Now is the time to look back at the notes you made when you completed your initial inventory of your papers and decide which of these categories meets the standards you established in the second stage of the planning process. If a category falls under the *keep* response, then make it into a category for your PDC. Cross out categories that didn't make the cut.

Steps to creating your Personal Data Collection (PDC):

- Determine what you have.
- Determine what rules should define what to keep in your PDC.
- Determine how you will classify, categorize, and arrange your documents.
- Sort, scan, and file your documents.
- Back up your digital system to protect from loss or damage.

Now review the names of your categories. When you look at the category, do you instantly know what it means (qualities 1 and 4)? Is the style of the naming convention consistent (quality 6)? For example, are you using names of companies for all of your vendors or are you using the names of your contacts at your vendors' businesses? Would a coworker be able to look at the category name and easily understand what is in the category (quality 3)? Can you easily add more categories to the list if you discover new information during the organizing process (quality 5)?

Are any of your categories too large and in need of division into subcategories? If you're thinking that you might have a category with thousands of entries, can you reduce the category into smaller units? If client X is the source of the majority of your work, then you might benefit from naming "Client X" as a main category and "Client X: Lease Agreements in California," "Client X: Lease Agreements in Texas," and "Client X: Lease Agreements in Massachusetts" as subcategories. Only you will be able to identify the categories of your work.

If you find yourself struggling with the category identification process, ask an organized coworker or someone in your company's HR department to review your ideas. If there is ever an emergency, these are the people who will be accessing your files, so getting their input now can be very helpful. Plus, these are the people who know what you do and have at least a vague understanding of how you do your work. Even if you're not struggling, these people can be terrific resources.

The final stage of your planning process will be to get your hands on the tools that you need to complete your paper and filing project. This is the least thought-intensive stage in the process.

The tools you need:

- Large horizontal surface

- Index cards or scrap paper

- Pens

- Shredder

- Recycling bin

- Trash can

- Document scanner

- Computer

- Empty file folders

- Label maker or printed labels

- Filing cabinet

Creating Order for Your Papers

The time has finally come to sort, scan, and transform your PDC into an orderly filing system. First things first: You don't have to begin and end this process in a single day. I know this assignment is scheduled only for today in this book, but many people benefit from setting aside a couple of hours a day over the course of a week or month to tackle this project. It's not a race. No one wins at organizing papers and files. (Although I would totally watch a speed-organizing Olympic event.) Second, on your way to creating order from chaos, it's okay if your office becomes more chaotic. Getting organized can be a messy process—but there is light at the end of the proverbial tunnel. Third, if you have a difficult time deciding if you should keep or get rid of a single document, my advice is to keep it. Six months from now you can go through a mini version of this process and purge and more precisely tweak your filing system.

Finally, here are a couple of helpful tips for people who have a bad habit of getting distracted while organizing. (You know, those times when you're supposed to be organizing something in your office but mysteriously find yourself in the break room.)

1. Create a pause barrier to help keep you in your office while you're organizing. Move your trash can so that it's in an awkward location near the exit. Don't block the pathway entirely, just put it in a place that makes you pause to wonder why it's there. When you see it, you'll think, "Oops! I'm supposed to be organizing my papers and files, not going to make jokes with the guys in the copy room."

2. Set an alarm to go off ten minutes after you start your project. When it beeps, assess what you've done and then hit the snooze button. When it goes off again, see if you've stayed on track during that chunk of time. Keep hitting the snooze button until you're in a groove and no longer need the reminder to stay on task.

Sorting

Remember the categories you determined for your filing system during the third stage of the planning process (pages 76–78)? Well, it's time to put them to use. Write the category names on separate sheets of scrap paper or index cards and spread them out over a large, horizontal surface like your office floor or a conference table. Now begin the tedious process of sorting all your papers into categorical piles. If a document doesn't have a home and doesn't belong in your PDC, then immediately shred it or toss it into the recycling bin. If it's a CYA or Extended Knowledge paper and it's good for you to keep, create a category index card for it and start a new pile.

What to shred? If you're looking to get rid of these documents, it's better to shred them than to put them directly into the recycling bin:

- Credit card applications
- Any piece of unwanted paper that contains: addresses, account numbers or access information, birth dates, budgets, photocopies of confidential documents, driver's license numbers, employment information, envelopes and address labels, estimates, expired legal papers, luggage tags, medical information, passwords, report cards, signatures, Social Security numbers, transcripts, travel itineraries, used airline tickets, and anything you wouldn't feel comfortable having a stranger read about you or your business
- Expired credit cards, bank cards, passports (after you get your new one), and identification cards (college, military, employee badges, etc.)
- Credit checks on vendors

During this process, you may also find that you have documents in your collection that belong in someone else's office. If this is the case, start a pile labeled with your coworker's name and put those papers into that pile. Later, when you're finished sorting, put a bow on the papers and deliver them to their rightful owner. Or if you find papers that belong in your filing system at home, make a *home* category and stack the papers there. Create a *work* category if you're doing this process at home and find office files.

To help remember what to do during this stage of the process, I came up with a ridiculous mnemonic device. The word I chose is SPECTRE, as in Silk Spectre from the *Watchmen* comic series. SPECTRE stands for:

- **S**ort and
- **P**ile
- **E**xtended knowledge and
- **C**YA papers, and
- **T**rash and
- **R**ecycle
- **E**verything else.

Scanning

Once you have finished sorting and/or purging all of your papers and files, it is time to decide what can become digital files and what needs to stay in physical form. If you own an art gallery or work in a recording studio, the contents of your PDC will look vastly different from a web programmer's or a teacher's collection. The theories and strategies I present can still work for you, but you may need to photograph three-dimensional objects instead of scanning them or make digital recordings of audio files. Items you need to keep in paper form might include signed contracts, notarized documents, receipts (especially if your company policy for reimbursements includes turning over a physical receipt for proof of payment), and legal proceedings filed with the court system. People often ask me whether they need to keep tax documents, and my response is to ask your corporate accountant. Tax laws for businesses change on a regular basis and a corporate accountant is going to have the most up-to-date and reliable information for you to follow. If you don't have one, get one. Being audited by the IRS will take more time and cost a lot more money than hiring an accountant.

If you're someone who conducts a lot of research, you'll find that scanning every article you read is a helpful researching tool. When you can remember reading something but don't remember exactly where you read it, you can search everything you've read with just one simple query on your computer. What you want to find will instantly appear.

Additionally, when magazines and journals are delivered to my office I immediately flip through them and pull out all the articles of interest to me. Afterward, I toss the publication into the recycling bin, scan the pulled-out pages, save the scans to a "to-read" folder on my hard drive, and read them when I have free time. This procedure gets rid of journal clutter in my office and also keeps the advertisements from tempting me to buy things I don't need.

There are a few of you reading this book who will refuse to scan a single document. This is completely fine, but, as I discussed earlier, a digital filing system makes it easier to find relationships among your files. Your filing system will still be incredibly useful, it just won't be your best alternative. On a more serious note, unless you keep your files in a fireproof and waterproof safe, they run the risk of being destroyed in a fire.

If you choose to scan your documents as recommended, use a scanner that has integrated OCR (optical character recognition) software. OCR software will read the text of the document and allow you to search your digital files for specific words and phrases—something you can't easily do with your papers in physical form.

Work your way through your piles individually and use this second sorting to create a file folder on your computer and, if needed, one for your filing cabinet. When creating your paper file, use a label maker to print the category name for your folder. I suggest using a label maker because the clarity of the print will speed up your retrieval time and the retrieval time of anyone else looking in your filing cabinet.

Filing

When establishing your new digital filing system, consider saving your scanned documents with descriptive file names that include date-, project-, and category-themed information. This style will help to make retrieval as simple as possible:

080507-boyd-evernote.txt

This document is an Unclutterer.com post about the Evernote software by Stowe Boyd and it ran on May 7, 2008. Whatever file-naming style you choose, be sure to be consistent (quality 6). I prefer this system because I can search for a file three different ways: by date, by author name, and by content. In my job, the date a post runs is different from when it was created, and the publishing date is what we find valuable. If all you need is a creation date, leave off the date code at the beginning of the file name since the creation date is saved as part of the file automatically.

Many document systems allow for tagging, meaning key words can be entered into the document that won't appear as text on a page but will help with searching and making connections among different files. Tagging is especially useful with images and other non-text-based files.

Also sort your digital files into the categories you established during the planning process. You will likely need to create subfolders that reflect your workflow, too. One fantastic example of how to do this comes from Brian Kieffer, one of

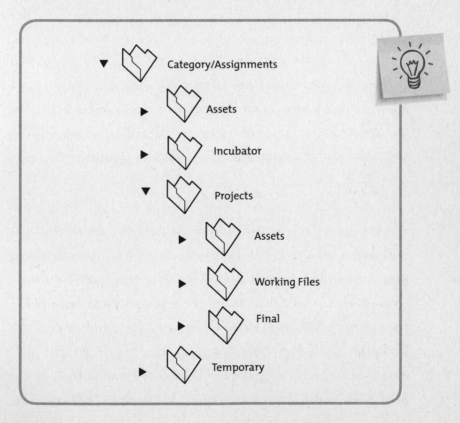

Unclutterer.com's suave programmers. Brian organizes folders on his computer for each of his clients (one of his categories), and each client folder contains three subfolders: "Assets," "Incubator," and "Projects." His "Assets" folder includes logos, correspondence, and software license information general to the referenced client. He uses the "Incubator" folder for ideas and research related to the client but not detailed to a specific project. Each subfolder within "Projects" is descriptively named and contains "Assets," "Working Files," and "Final." For example, he has a subfolder in his "Projects" folder named "Unclutterer" that contains all of his work for our website.

You're bound to find yourself working on documents or files that don't need to be stored indefinitely on your computer. Many people benefit from having a "Temporary" folder in each of their "Project" files. Decide on a date when you will purge the files contained in the folder. Take five minutes to clean out the folder at the end of every workweek. Just be careful not to keep files for a number of weeks without opening them and establishing why you're still holding on to them.

Earlier in the chapter, I mentioned that a digital filing system can allow one file to appear in multiple locations. You can create these links by making shortcuts or aliases in folders that aren't the primary location of a file. Shortcuts are one of the most useful yet underused organizational tools for an uncluttered computer. Suppose you have a project that requires the use of a client's logo. Of course, you can create a copy of all the client's logo treatments from the client's "Assets" folder. But then you would have to remember to update two files whenever the logo changes. Instead, you can create a shortcut for the logo file and place the shortcut in the "Assets" folder on your desktop instead. The same file is now effectively in two places at once.

To create a shortcut on a PC, right-click (for Mac users, control-click) on a file. If you're using a PC, choose "Create Shortcut" from the drop-down menu. A shortcut will be created that you can drag to any location on your computer. If you're using a Mac, choose "Make Alias" from the drop-down menu. Again, an alias will be created that you can drag to any location on your computer.

If you aren't fond of using a hierarchical filing structure on your computer or want to boost the speed with which you access information, consider installing a third-party desktop search engine to explore your digital files. I have found that Google Desktop (desktop.google.com) is beefy enough for all of my search needs, and it's free to download. If you want something even more robust, check out Copernic Desktop Search (copernic.com), but be prepared to pay for it if you want to use it at work. Currently, a bare-bones version of Copernic Desktop Search is free, but only for noncommercial use.

Organizing Old Systems

If you have a slew of old files on your computer, group all of them together and dump them into an "Archive" folder. This approach will allow you to get a fresh start without losing your old data. The files are still there if you need them, but they're out of the way. Once your new system is up and working, you can wade through and fix the files you've put into "Archive" as time permits. If it is your physical filing cabinet that has a mess of old files, you will want to sort, scan, and refile the documents to fit into your new system.

Protecting Your System

Now that you have taken the time to organize your files, back up all of your digital data. If you work in an office with a business-wide network, check with your IT department to see if it is already being done for you. If you work from home, run your own business, or are just interested in learning how to properly back up your data for personal reasons, keep reading this section.

Hard drives have a bad habit of dying, and they usually decide to call it quits at the most inconvenient moments. To avoid losing all your digital data, back up your data using online storage and two external drives that you can swap daily. If a fire or another natural disaster destroys your office, you will be very happy that you had the off-site backup. If you're worried about security, encrypt the data before uploading it online. (Be sure to check with your company's IT department to make sure that you aren't violating any policies by using an online backup storage method.) And be sure to give your user name, password, and encryption key to a trusted coworker or your company's HR department for your employee file.

I keep an external drive connected to my computer at all times and swap it out nightly. This backup is for quick retrieval of files I might accidentally delete over the course of a day or if the internal hard drive on my computer fails.

These two backup methods make losing important digital data nearly impossible.

Tuesday Evening: Household Chores Aren't Just for Children

Coming home and using your Reception Station for the first time was hopefully a welcome relief after a long day at work. This welcome home routine keeps junk mail and trash from entering your home and sets the stage for the next time you need to leave—no more lost keys, rotten lunches in your child's backpack, or pocket change ending up in your washing machine. But going through this routine was only a preview of your less stressful life. Tonight you're going to focus on putting more routines into action to make it even easier for you at home. Tonight's work is the foundation for creating a space that you always look forward to coming home to.

Once you're home, eating dinner and spending the rest of the evening in front of the television seems like a decent reward after all the scanning, shredding, sorting, and filing you did at work. Chores are the last thing on your mind when it comes to things you want to do. But if you spend just thirty minutes an evening doing chores efficiently, your weekends will be mostly free for relaxing and doing whatever you want. You won't have to worry about an endless amount of laundry, dishes, or messes taking shape in your home.

Creating Cues

I know teachers who flip their classroom lights off and on when they want their students to be quiet. When a fire alarm sounds in a public space, people leave the building. When a traffic light turns red, drivers put on their cars' brakes. A cue is the first stage of a conditioned reflex that signals your brain to start an activity, and I've found that cues work wonders to motivate me to do chores.

A music playlist can work to get you moving for activities you might not love to do (e.g., cleaning, exercise, laundry). When you hit the play button on the playlist, you hear the first song and know that it's time to do some chores. That first song causes you to think, "X happens next." When I started using cues, it took me a couple of weeks to train myself, but now it's just second nature.

When I hear Dee-Lite's song "Groove Is in the Heart," I want to start cleaning. "Flux" by Bloc Party motivates me to get work done after lunch when I'm sleepy. A dance version of Kanye West's "Stronger" encourages me to exercise.

I realize that the idea of cues and conditioned responses is a bit abnormal compared to other antiprocrastination advice, but—nontraditional or not—cues work. If you have difficulty finding motivation to do chores, create cues to help you get moving.

Establishing and Maintaining Routines

I love exploring and encountering new things, places, and flavors. But I also find comfort in routines. After traveling for more than a few days, it's so nice to come home to sleep in my familiar bed. When I can have both variety and routine in my life, I feel content and happy. In many ways, it's the routines that make the variety possible.

At the end of the last chapter I briefly touched on the topic of routines in regard to your home's Reception Station. I also briefly mentioned laundry being a regular part of your week, but now it's time to discuss how you might set up your laundry routine. When and how you do your laundry will depend on whether you need to go to a Laundromat to wash your clothes or if you live in a home with a washer and dryer. If you need to use a Laundromat, schedule two hours on a weeknight, every other week, to take care of this chore (Laundromats are usually less crowded on weeknights). I've had a number of friends who live in washing machine–free apartments tell me that they have had great success taking their laundry once a week to a fluff 'n' fold. They pay a nominal fee in addition to the cost of using the machines themselves to have someone else wash and dry their clothes. Since I have a washer and dryer in my house, I've never tried these services. But if you have the extra money and no on-site laundry facilities, this is a fantastic, efficient idea.

If you're like me and have a washer and dryer in your home,

spread your laundry routine out over the week to stay on top of it. In my family of two, we do laundry on Mondays and Thursdays. We wash our clothes (usually two or three loads: whites, colors, and delicates) on Monday nights and bedsheets and towels (usually two loads, as our machine has a small drum) on Thursday nights. If the hampers are full on Thursday, we'll do a load of clothes on Thursday night after we're done with the sheets and towels. A family of four (or more) probably can't get by doing laundry so rarely. Consider the following routine for larger families:

- Monday: Launder all the sheets from the beds.

- Tuesday: Launder children's clothing.

- Wednesday: Launder adults' clothing.

- Thursday: Launder towels.

- Friday: Launder children's clothing.

- Saturday: Launder adults' clothing.

- Sunday: Rest.

General house-cleaning routines require a nightly commitment but don't need to be overwhelming. Set aside thirty minutes—and not a single minute more—per evening to accomplish what you need to keep your house maintained. I prefer to do my thirty minutes immediately after work, but I can definitely see how others might want to wait to do chores until after dinner. It doesn't matter when you do them, just that you do them.

I like to play one of my playlists while I'm doing general chores. Music with 150 or more beats per minute helps me to keep moving at a quick pace. I also like my playlist to be as close to thirty minutes as possible, so that I get the signal when it's time to stop working.

Like I mentioned earlier, these thirty minutes on weeknights will free you from having to spend your weekends cleaning your home. You'll have two full, glorious weekend days to focus on what matters most to you. Spend the first ten minutes doing a general pickup throughout the house and then the last twenty minutes focusing your efforts on a specific space. It seems like a lot, but when you're working the time goes by very quickly. To get started, designate different rooms for each day of the week, such as:

- Monday: Kitchen and dining room

- Tuesday: Bathroom(s)

- Wednesday: Bedroom(s)

- Thursday: Living and family rooms

- Friday: Other spaces (garage, Reception Station, hallways, etc.)

If you have children, a roommate(s), a spouse, or a parent(s) living with you, everyone should work together on the house during this time. The more helping hands you have, the less time it will take to get your home into shape. Also, when everyone is working together, it makes the process more enjoyable.

In the Friday chapter, I'll explore routines for your office, which will cover office chores. One piece of related advice that I want to mention here is that you should have designated times to clear everything off your desk. If you work from home, this task should be done every day—file papers, pay bills, put away supplies, clear out your inbox, etc. If you work outside of your home, you might be able to get by doing this chore in your home office just once a week.

In the Thursday chapter, I'll talk in detail about kitchen routines. Meal planning, preparation, and cleanup are so large of a topic that they get their own specific section in the book. A few routines worth mentioning here are cleaning up immediately after every meal (dishes cleaned or put into the dishwasher, counters wiped, and all ingredients returned to their cupboards) and regular shopping. People who have kitchens with a decent amount of storage should have a weekly appointment with the grocery store. If storage is limited in your space, you might prefer the method of stopping by the market to pick up fresh foods every night after work. Regardless of the shopping routine you choose to use, it should be planned on your schedule. One final routine is to sort through all of the items in your pantry at least twice a year. You can do it when you change your clocks for daylight savings time and when you switch them back again. Toss out any item past its expiration date.

As previously mentioned in the Monday chapter, don't forget to sort through your wardrobe at the end of every season and get rid of any clothes you didn't wear during that time. Check your towels and linens to make sure that they're in decent shape, too.

Finally, you might also want to put routines in place to un-clutter your car (a quick pass every time you get out of it and a weekly, more intense review), your yard (mowing, raking, shoveling), and other rooms you might have in your home (wine cellar, exercise room, basement). Think about your home and all the things you can create routines for to keep it in tip-top shape. On pages 98–99, I've created a chart showing how you might complete the chores over the course of a week. Modify the chart to fit your needs, and follow the schedule you create.

Running Errands

Errands and chores are the same thing, in my opinion. They take time and need to be done to make life run smoothly. I try to limit errands to two days a week so that I'm not always on the go. If you have more people in your home, you might need to add a third day into the mix.

I run errands on Tuesday evenings and Saturday mornings. I keep a box with a lid on it in my Reception Station where I put objects that need to be repaired, dropped off, or serviced in some way and notes about stops I need to make (like grocery lists). When I run errands, I grab the box and head out the door. I like to work from the farthest stop to the closest stop from my home. It's nice to be near home when you finish your errands instead of half an hour away in another town. Regular errands for me include going to the bank, post office, gas station, and grocery store. The post office and grocery store are on my Tuesday-evening runs and the bank and gas station are my regular Saturday-morning errands.

Think about the errands you typically run, and consider lumping them together instead of running some every night. If you live with someone else, consider having one person run errands on Tuesday evenings and the other run them on Saturday mornings. Unless you're a professional errand runner, you shouldn't have to waste your life running around town.

Hiring Help

There are times when life can be so hectic that running to others for help may be the best solution for keeping your sanity, especially if you've budgeted for such emergencies. This can be an annual, quarterly, or weekly occurrence—it's really about what helps you when you need or want it.

Three ways hiring help can save you time and energy:

1. *Messenger Services.* In many large communities, there are companies established to provide personal assistants and errand runners at hourly rates. A Google search of your area might turn up a list of names. Use companies that are bonded and have adequate insurance for your items (not doing so puts you and your property at risk). Also, feel comfortable checking out customer reviews and references. Messenger services are nice options for running packages and envelopes across town at minimal fees.

2. *Grocery Services.* When I was regularly working more than sixty-five hours a week, I used a grocery delivery service. The service

had an online ordering system; it initially took about an hour to set up my first order. Subsequent orders were much faster to enter since the program remembered all of my previous purchases and created a checklist I could zoom through in less than five minutes. Check with the grocery stores in your community to see whether any offer delivery services. The savings I made on time were worth the charges for delivery and tip. If your favorite store doesn't deliver, they might have a similar pickup service where all you have to do is swing by the store, pay for your order, and load the groceries into your car.

3. *House-cleaning Services*. These services can also help to keep your home in order. Some services clean your home from top to bottom, while others just do specific areas like floors or bathrooms. Ask for estimates from a number of different companies to get an idea of the range of services and fees. Again, a cleaning company should be properly insured and you should feel comfortable with any service provider who comes into your home.

Charting It Out

The following is a standard weekly routine that I'm providing as a reference. Review your specific circumstances and create a routine that works for your needs. If your house is small, you might be able to shorten this schedule. If you have many children, you might need to beef it up. This isn't a law, its just a jumping-off point to get you thinking about the routines for your home:

Monday	Tuesday	Wednesday

Morning Routine (1 hr)
Shower and get ready
Breakfast prep, eating,
  and cleanup
	Morning Routine (1 hr)
	Shower and get ready
	Breakfast prep, eating,
	  and cleanup
		Morning Routine (1 hr)
		Shower and get ready
		Breakfast prep, eating,
		  and cleanup

Work	**Work**	**Work**
	Errand Running (1.5 hr) Grocery shopping Post office	

Welcome Home Routine
  (approx 10 min)
Sort and shred mail
Empty pockets and bags
Set up for morning
Process receipts,
  papers, lunch boxes, etc.
	Welcome Home Routine
	  (approx 10 min)
	Sort and shred mail
	Empty pockets and bags
	Set up for morning
	Process receipts,
	  papers, lunch boxes, etc.
		Welcome Home Routine
		  (approx 10 min)
		Sort and shred mail
		Empty pockets and bags
		Set up for morning
		Process receipts,
		  papers, lunch boxes, etc.

Laundry Routine (30 min) Clothes		

Dinner Routine
  (45 min)
Prep, eating, clean up
	Dinner Routine
	  (45 min)
	Prep, eating, clean up
		Dinner Routine
		  (45 min)
		Prep, eating, clean up

General Cleaning
  (30 min)
House pickup
Kitchen and dining
  room—including meal
  planning, grocery list
  making, etc.
	General Cleaning
	  (30 min)
	House pickup
	Bathroom(s)
		General Cleaning
		  (30 min)
		House pickup
		Bedroom(s)

Before Bed Routine
  (20 min)
Change into pajamas
Pick out clothes for
  tomorrow
Make tomorrow's lunches
Feed pets
Get ready for bed
Secure doors and win-
  dows
Turn off lights
	Before Bed Routine
	  (20 min)
	Change into pajamas
	Pick out clothes for
	  tomorrow
	Make tomorrow's lunches
	Feed pets
	Get ready for bed
	Secure doors and win-
	  dows
	Turn off lights
		Before Bed Routine
		  (20 min)
		Change into pajamas
		Pick out clothes for
		  tomorrow
		Make tomorrow's lunches
		Feed pets
		Get ready for bed
		Secure doors and win-
		  dows
		Turn off lights

Thursday	Friday	Saturday	Sunday

Morning Routine (1 hr)
Shower and get ready
Breakfast prep, eating,
   and cleanup
	Morning Routine (1 hr)
	Shower and get ready
	Breakfast prep, eating,
	   and cleanup
		Morning Routine (1 hr)
		Shower and get ready
		Breakfast prep, eating,
		   and cleanup
			Morning Routine (1 hr)
			Shower and get ready
			Breakfast prep, eating,
			   and cleanup

Work	Work		
		Errand Running (20 min) Bank Gas station	

Welcome Home Routine
   (approx 10 min)
Sort and shred mail
Empty pockets and bags
Set up for morning
Process receipts, papers,
   lunch boxes, etc.
	Welcome Home Routine
	   (approx 10 min)
	Sort and shred mail
	Empty pockets and bags
	Set up for morning
	Process receipts, papers,
	   lunch boxes, etc.		

Laundry Routine (30 min) Sheets and towels			

Dinner Routine
   (45 min)
Prep, eating, clean up
	Dinner Routine
	   (45 min)
	Prep, eating, clean up		

General Cleaning
   (30 min)
House pickup
Living and family
   rooms
	General Cleaning (30 min)
	House pickup
	Other areas that may
	   need attention: Recep-
	   tion Station, garage,
	   hallways, car, pet areas,
	   or yard		

Before Bed Routine
   (20 min)
Change into pajamas
Pick out clothes for
   tomorrow
Make tomorrow's
   lunches
Feed pets
Get ready for bed
Secure doors and
   windows
Turn off lights
	Before Bed Routine
	   (20 min)
	Change into pajamas
	Pick out clothes for to-
	   morrow
	Feed pets
	Get ready for bed
	Secure doors and
	   windows
	Turn off lights
		Before Bed Routine
		   (20 min)
		Change into pajamas
		Pick out clothes for
		   tomorrow
		Feed pets
		Get ready for bed
		Secure doors and
		   windows
		Turn off lights
			Before Bed Routine
			   (20 min)
			Change into pajamas
			Pick out clothes for
			   tomorrow
			Make tomorrow's
			   lunches
			Feed pets
			Get ready for bed
			Secure doors and
			   windows
			Turn off lights

Fall Cleaning Guide

Fall Cleaning for the Busy Person

☐ 1. Change your furnace filters.

☐ 2. Replace batteries in your smoke and carbon monoxide detectors and test them.

☐ 3. Check fire extinguishers.

☐ 4. Clean leaves and debris out of gutters.

☐ 5. Drain gasoline from lawn mower.

☐ 6. Set out snow shovel and a plastic tray to hold winter shoes.

☐ 7. Put ice scraper in car and a warm blanket in the trunk.

Kitchen

☐ 8. Scrub floors and counters.

☐ 9. Clean refrigerator and freezer with a mild detergent.

☐ 10. Check expiration dates and dispose of expired food in refrigerator and pantry.

Bathroom

☐ 11. Toss expired makeup, liquids, and supplies.

Bedroom

☐ 12. Wash mattress pad, bed skirt, and comforter.

☐ 13. Wash warm-weather blankets and store in plastic until spring.

☐ 14. Swap out warmer-weather clothing for cooler-weather clothing.

Dining room and living room

☐ 15. Move furniture and vacuum or sweep where furniture had been.

Home office

☐ 16. Move furniture and vacuum or sweep where furniture had been.

☐ 17. Clean desk.

☐ 18. Wipe down telephone.

Exterior spaces

☐ 19. Clean outdoor furniture and store for winter.

☐ 20. Rake leaves and branches from yard.

☐ 21. Unhook garden hoses and drain water.

Other

☐ 22. Properly dispose of expired medicines (page 61).

Fall Cleaning for the Dedicated Cleaner

☐ 23. Items 1–22.

☐ 24. Inspect and clean fireplace.

☐ 25. Vacuum out dryer hose and scrub the lint trap on washing machine.

☐ 26. Remove, clean, and store window screens and replace with storm windows.

☐ 27. Dust light fixtures and ceiling fans.

☐ 28. Take trash cans and litter boxes to self-service car wash and power wash.

☐ 29. Review paper filing system (page 70).

☐ 30. Inspect tile and wood floors and repair any damage.

Kitchen

☐ 31. Clean cabinets and drawers.

☐ 32. Inspect tableware for damage and replace any damaged pieces.

☐ 33. If necessary, defrost freezer.

☐ 34. Clean inside of oven, stove burners, and range hood.

☐ 35. Pull refrigerator out from wall and wash floor underneath. Vacuum its coils.

Bathroom

☐ 36. Clean showerhead.

Bedroom

☐ 37. Clean summer shoes and take repairs to cobbler.

Dining room

☐ 38. Clean sideboard and drawers.

Computers and electronics

☐ 39. Clean each item per manufacturer's instructions.

☐ 40. Go through digital files and organize data (page 84).

Exterior spaces

☐ 41. Replace doormats if needed.

☐ 42. Inspect pesticides and properly dispose of containers that are leaking or expired.

Other

☐ 43. Clean and store summer sports equipment.

☐ 44. Clean pet toys, food bowls, and accoutrements.

Fall Cleaning for the Overachiever

☐ 45. Items 1–44.

☐ 46. Scrub lint trap on washing machine.

☐ 47. Inspect garage door opener and belt.

☐ 48. Inspect all floors and wax or steam clean.

☐ 49. Inspect walls for scuffs or damage and fix.

☐ 50. Oil door hinges.

Kitchen

☐ 51. Clean exteriors of small appliances.

☐ 52. Polish and/or season pots and pans.

Bathroom

☐ 53. Launder shower curtain and replace liner if mildewy.

Bedroom

☐ 54. Flip mattress, if recommended by the manufacturer.

☐ 55. Clean jewelry per manufacturer's instructions.

Dining room

☐ 56. Polish wood furniture.

☐ 57. Polish and/or dust display items.

Living room

☐ 58. Wash slipcovers and steam clean upholstered furniture.

☐ 59. Polish furniture and tables.

☐ 60. Dust books and bookshelves.

Exterior spaces

☐ 61. Clean porches and patios.

chapter 4

Wednesday

Wednesday is the day when you're fully immersed in the hustle and bustle of your life. You've accomplished some things, but you still have a lot to do before you reach the weekend. Being organized and uncluttered will help you glide through these busy times when you're caught up with things to do and places to be.

Without clutter and chaos, you sleep well because you don't have stress weighing on your mind. You wake up refreshed and ready to face the day. Your interactions with other people are enjoyable, calm, and collected. You look forward to sharing meals with your family and friends. Even though you're active, there is a comfortable flow to your day.

Today's projects are focused on handling the stresses that pop up every workday—navigating around an accident on the way to work, dealing with misinterpreted e-mails, and figuring out what to serve for an unexpected dinner party. Organizing and uncluttering your bedroom, commute, communication processes, and kitchen can reduce the chaos. They're small steps with giant rewards.

Wednesday Morning: Your Bedroom and Commute

Your bedroom is where you renew and pamper yourself. Of all the rooms in your home, your bedroom should be the most relaxing of all. There should be as few distractions as possible. All you need is a bed with a comfortable mattress, clean sheets, warm blankets, fluffy pillows, and a nightstand to hold your alarm clock. The room should be free of clutter, stress, and essentially anything that does not promote rest and rejuvenation (well, except for that awful alarm clock).

Restorative sleep is essential to a remarkable life. When you're exhausted you have difficulty concentrating, you move slowly, you're easily agitated, you stop thinking reasonably, you don't make it to work on time, and you ignore chores and routines because you don't have enough energy to do them. But when you are well rested, you can handle anything that life sends your way.

Work-life symbiosis is impossible without a good night's sleep.

Keep this truth in mind as you take on your next project. This morning, you're going to unclutter your bedroom and your commute to work.

Unclutter Your Bedroom

Clear your bedroom of anything that doesn't promote sleep. Your floors, dresser tops, and nightstands should be free of all clutter. Nothing should be on your bed except for sheets, blankets, and pillows. Artwork and decor elements should be calming. Clothes, jewelry, and shoes need to be stored in their proper places. And, by all means, don't have a television or a computer in your bedroom. Televisions and computers stimulate your mind and have nothing to do with sleep. This room is your sanctuary and your retreat from the demands of the world.

Be careful that you don't go overboard with pillows. A slew of decorative pillows can be clutter if you're wasting time taking them off and putting them back on the bed every day.

Your nightstand should have a drawer or drawers in it so that you can keep tissues, books, and other things inside of it instead of on top of it. Use dividers to separate the contents of the drawer(s) so that you don't have to hunt for things in the dark.

If you live in a small space, you may need to dedicate the area under your bed to storage of out-of-season clothing and bed linens. If you do this, be sure to use a bed skirt that touches the floor so that you don't see the items when you're moving around the room. Also, use clear plastic bins with tightly fitting lids so that dust and bugs don't find their way into your stored items.

Sorting Through Bed Linens

Sheets and blankets are similar to towels in that they are often concealed clutter in our homes. They are used for years and then take up permanent residence in the linen closet once they're removed from regular circulation. We hold on to them, thinking that maybe, one day, we'll have reason to use them again for a picnic or an occasional trip to the beach. When I went through my first clutter-purging process, I found three sets of twin bedsheets in my linen storage. I hadn't owned a twin bed since college. Those sheets made it through five moves, across more than a thousand miles, and I had zero use for them. When I uncluttered my linen closet, I packed them up and donated them to my local animal shelter.

If you live in a four-season climate, all you need are four sets of sheets for your bed: two warm-weather sheet sets (cotton) and two cold-weather sheet sets (flannel or jersey). If you live in a consistent climate, you really only need to own two sets of sheets. The idea is that you have one set of sheets on your bed and one set ready to go on laundry day. Off-season sheets should be stored in a sealed container waiting for their alternate season. You don't need more than one set of sheets for a guest bed, and you may not even need those if the bed is the same size as another bed in your home.

Good sheets should:

1. appropriately fit the bed even after many launderings,

2. have properly functioning elastic,

3. be hole and stain free,

4. be made of a soft and durable single-ply cotton with a thread count between two hundred and four hundred for your warm-weather sheets, and

5. allow you to be comfortable so that you can sleep soundly.

While we're on the topic, you should know that sheets that claim to be one thousand thread count are usually a scam. If you look closely at the packaging, you'll see that it says "two-ply" or "four-ply" on the label. This means that the manufacturer is counting plys of threads, not actual threads. Single plys are more durable and usually softer. According to *Consumer Reports:*[7]

> The right way to count is to add up all vertical and horizontal threads in a square inch of fabric. Two hundred is typical and perfectly fine; 400 may provide a finer, softer sheet. Above 400, the only difference is likely to be price . . . Bottom line: Pick a sheet between 200 and 400 thread count that meets your other criteria. Paying more for higher thread count is wasting money.

Another idea: To speed up the bed-making process in the morning, stop using a top sheet and instead use a duvet with a cover that is easy to launder.

Organizing for Better Sleep and Waking Up

With a luxurious mattress, supportive pillows, soft sheets, and blankets on your bed, and your room free of all distractions, you will immediately notice an improvement in your quality of sleep. The following are additional tips to help you sleep soundly and wake up refreshed and on time in the morning:

- *Get ready for bed an hour before you go to bed.* I mentioned this suggestion in the Monday chapter, but it's worth mentioning again. Changing into your pajamas when you still have energy keeps dirty clothes off the bedroom floor. It also sends a signal to your brain that it's time to settle down and prepare for sleep.

- *Maintain a schedule.* Going to bed and waking up at the same time every day establishes a routine and rhythm for your body. When you're getting adequate sleep, you won't need to bank sleep on the weekends.

- *Keep a sleep journal.* If you don't know how much sleep you need to function at your best, keep a log of when you go to bed, when you wake up, and how you feel that day. I need a minimum of nine hours of sleep a night but less than ten (if I get more than ten, I'm groggy all day). Learn about your needs from the information in your journal.

- *Stick to a routine.* At the end of every day, you should have an established routine to make sure you are ready for a relaxing night's sleep and are set for the morning. Your pre-sleep routine might include tucking your children into bed, changing into your pajamas, picking out clothes for tomorrow, washing your face, brushing your teeth, assembling lunches, locking doors and securing windows, checking your Reception Station and making sure everything is where it needs to be, turning off lights and electronic equipment, setting your alarm, and crawling into bed.

- *Commit to a clutter-free space.* An overflowing laundry hamper can create stress, objects on your bed can limit your mobility when you're sleeping, and shoes strewn about the floor can cause injury as you're getting in and out of bed. At the first sign of clutter in this space, stop what you're doing and clean it up. Don't let anything interfere with your sleep.

If you repeatedly wake up feeling more tired than you did when you went to bed, or if you have to set multiple alarms to wake up in the morning, you need to talk to your doctor. You may be consuming too much caffeine, your thyroid could be in overdrive or underperforming, you could be suffering from depression, your body might need more exercise, or you could have a sleep disorder. Your doctor will be able to monitor your sleep behaviors and determine why you're not able to get the sleep you need.

Getting Out the Door

You probably have a couple of coworkers who are chronically late to work by at least fifteen minutes. Or maybe you're the one who is always behind schedule. Whether it's you or someone else, the whole team suffers when even just one person doesn't arrive on time. In many offices, it's also cause for being fired. Sure, there are a few times a year when you or someone else will have to call in late to work because of an emergency or uncontrollable circumstance. But it becomes a problem when you are late more than twice a month, or you show up late and don't call in to your boss or coworkers about it. As an employer, I find both behaviors unacceptable. Punctuality and courtesy are two of the most basic components of holding a job.

Chronic lateness could be considered a sign that you don't care about keeping your job. If you're only late to work and nowhere else, you should talk to someone (a career counselor, therapist, mentor, or trusted friend) about how you might be able to change your current work situation. If this is far from the case, and you want to keep your job, you need to figure out why you're repeatedly arriving late to work. Create a log to record the following activity and scheduling information for one week:

Activity	Time Sample	Time Your Answer
When are you going to bed?	11:00 PM	
What time are you setting your alarm for in the morning?	7:00 AM	
What time are you actually getting out of bed?	7:21 AM	
What time do you need to be at work?	8:30 AM	
How long does it take you to get ready (shower, shave, brush teeth, get dressed)?	40 min	
How long does it take you to fix, eat, and clean up breakfast?	20 min	
What other responsibilities do you have in the morning and how long does it take you to complete them?	Take dog on walk— 10 min	
How long does it usually take you to get to work?	20 min	
What time should you leave the house in the morning?	8:10 AM	
How many hours of sleep do you need a night to perform your best?	9 hours	
What adjustments should you make to arrive at work on time?	Go to bed by 10:00 PM so that I'm out of bed at 7:00 AM	

Once you have determined how long it actually takes you to complete your morning routine, you can find the places where the process can be improved. Are you hitting the snooze alarm five times each morning because you're exhausted? If this is the case, you need to break yourself of that habit by going to bed earlier. Experience has taught me that to get out of bed just fifteen minutes earlier each morning, most people need to go to bed thirty minutes earlier. To wake up and feel refreshed thirty minutes earlier in the morning requires going to bed a full hour earlier.

If you have children and are responsible for getting them ready in the morning, I want you to imagine the worst morning you have ever had with your child. Did he forget to tell you that you needed to make him a costume for the school play? Were there disagreements over what she wanted to wear? Every morning, you need to be prepared for the worst but hope for the best. Plan for what I call Child-Inspired Disruptions in your schedule. For most people, the Child-Inspired Disruption rarely takes more than fifteen minutes, so you should schedule an extra fifteen minutes of nothing into every morning. Things tend to go more smoothly if the adults in the house are completely ready by the time the kids get out of bed. You can sit back and read the paper if no one needs your help, or you can respond to whatever emergency arises. Having the extra fifteen minutes in your morning schedule is also a good idea if you don't have children.

Commuting to the Office

After waking up on time and getting ready on schedule, your next step is to get to work by the time you're expected to be there.

When it comes to commuting, walking is the best form of transportation. There are rarely delays or disruptions because you are in complete control of when you leave your place and when you arrive at work. But walking isn't realistic for most people.

If instead you drive alone, take public transportation, bike, fly, carpool, or use a combination of these methods, you are probably looking for ways to make this process more predictable, organized, and enjoyable. The following tips and tricks will get you to work on time:

- *Be prepared.* When an accident, construction, or some other delay-inducing event pops up on your route, you're going to want an exit strategy. Use a GPS or Google Maps to navigate back roads *before* you need to use them. If you're using public transportation, find ways to walk between all of the stops on your route or places where your bus might meet a subway stop or even where to get off the express train and onto the local. Learning these alternate routes also can help to break up the monotony of your regular commute.

- *Collect information.* Tune in to what is happening before you leave your house. Some television and radio stations have personal alerts that can be sent to your e-mail account. Check out your station's website and/or broadcast and learn as much as you can about what to expect on the roads, rails, and public transportation routes.

- *Read the signs.* Announcements about public transportation delays in service are posted a few days in advance.

Check the notices to plan ahead so you're not caught off guard by a service interruption. Check your county, city, state, or public transportation website for up-to-date information.

- *Get to know people's names.* If you catch the same bus every day, strike up a casual acquaintance with your bus driver. Say hello, smile, and learn his name. If you're running late, he might be more likely to wait for you as you run to catch him. I'm not making any promises, but the extra effort never hurts.

- *Master your route.* Know which train cars are closest to your exit and preferred stairs. Know which lanes have the fewest merges and usually move the fastest. Time different routes and learn which ones are more likely to experience delays, have more stoplights, or have lower volume on certain days of the week.

- *Always travel in HOV lanes.* In many metropolitan areas, there are programs to match passengers and drivers who want to take advantage of high-occupancy vehicle (HOV) lanes. Check out ride-share programs (erideshare.com) and talk to your HR department about access to van and car pools. Large cities may have slug-line communities you might wish to consider. "Slugs" (passengers) line up in designated areas and drivers simply pull up next to the line and accept passengers. Do a web search for your city and the phrase "slug line" to find the website for your community.

Consuming Media While Commuting

One of the advantages to having a long commute, especially when someone else is doing the driving, is that you have time to work and gather information. If you subscribe to your local newspaper, you can read it while you ride. You also can type up a report on your laptop, send text messages and e-mails, or crack open a book.

I recommend traveling with a smart phone or an iPod when you're going to be on public transportation for more than half an hour. A smart phone (like an iPhone) enables you to listen to music or an audiobook, play a game, read an ebook, or surf the web. Smart phones and iPods are small, light, and take up considerably less space in your bag than a newspaper, book, gaming system, and laptop do. They're space saving, time saving, organized, and fun.

There are thousands of services that can help to keep you productive during your commute. The following are just a handful of programs I have found to improve the quality of a commuting experience:

- *Audiobooks.* You can purchase digital audiobooks from iTunes, audible.com, and other book retail websites. You can also download audiobooks from your local library and listen to them for a limited time (usually two or three weeks). To learn if your library has this program, go to search.overdrive.com.

- *Ebooks.* Visual processors often don't enjoy listening to au-diobooks and prefer to use their eyes instead of their ears to consume text. If you fall into this category, buy a Kindle or Sony eBook Reader. Or, if you have an iPhone, down-load the Stanza and Kindle applications. All of these pro-grams let you read books digitally, and you don't have to worry about a physical book becoming clutter in your home after you finish reading it.

- *Instapaper.* Throughout my workday, I come across doz-ens of websites and articles online that I want to read but not at that exact moment. For these times, I've installed a program called Instapaper (instapaper.com) on my com-puter and smart phone. The program adds a button to my browser that says "Read Later." When you press this but-ton, the program saves the page and adds it to a list of un-read items. Sync your smart phone and your computer to share information between devices. To access your unread items, pull up the application and read the pages when you have the time on your commute. You don't have to be online to read the articles, which makes it great for under-ground and air travel.

- *Slingbox.* Some of the best television programs are on at very inconvenient times of the day. If you aren't driving, watch these recorded shows during your commute on your smart phone or laptop with the help of a Slingbox. Hook up a Slingbox to your cable box or DVR and access your recorded shows over the Internet or data network. This is also great to use if you work out on a treadmill, elliptical machine, or stationary bike—you can catch up on television shows when it's convenient for you.

Having an organized and productive sleep routine, bedroom, wake-up schedule, and commute will help you start your busy day without extra stress and frustration. By Wednesday, your body needs to be relaxed and refreshed to sustain the energy you need to make it through the rest of the week. The more uncluttered you are, the easier things will be.

Wednesday at Work: Communication Processes

Every business, big or small, needs to communicate its message to its intended audience. Widgets won't sell if no one knows that widgets are for sale. Projects can't be completed if teams don't communicate their goals. Cogs can never be improved if the cog company doesn't listen to its consumers. Communication is at the heart of every job, and being able to do it well and efficiently can give you an advantage in the workplace.

The Four Types of Meetings

I used to work for an organization that could have been aptly named We Love Meetings. My business cards should have read Erin Rooney, Meeting Attendee. I went to three to five hours of meetings every workday, although most of the time I had no reason to be in the meetings. There were no agendas, presenters would read word-for-word from their PowerPoint slides, and rarely was anything decided. After ten months, I gave notice and found a new job. Try not to be surprised, but the organization no longer exists.

Hundreds of meetings later, I've concluded that there are only four times when a meeting is appropriate:

1. *Shareholders' and/or Board of Directors' Meetings.* Based on the size and structure of your business or organization, these meetings may be required by law. If you need to have these meetings, then by all means, have them and stay out of jail.

2. *Untethered Brainstorming Meetings.* Creative idea generation is essential to every organization. An organized brainstorming meeting can be an amazing gift to a company. Keep attendance to ten people or fewer, and it's best if the issue to be brainstormed is e-mailed to everyone at least twenty-four hours before the meeting. This gives people time to think about the issue before arriving at the meeting. It may also be helpful to have someone who is not part of the discussion act as a moderator. Discussion should be lively (maybe even heated) and focus on ideas instead of people. At Unclutterer.com, our pitch meetings are held in this fashion.

3. *Off-Site Strategy Meetings.* These meetings are most productive with teams of ten or fewer people and everyone on the team present. An agenda should be circulated at least twenty-four hours in advance of the meeting. Each item on the agenda should be focused on overarching strategies within the organization or team building. Avoid presentations, and instead aim for push-up-your-sleeves-type discussions. Use a timer and a moderator to help keep attendees focused. I've found success in telling everyone to bring nothing but themselves and their favorite coffee mug or water bottle to the meetings (no laptops, no PDAs, no BlackBerries). A blank notebook and pen are then furnished to each attendee at the start of the first session. Exemptions to this rule might be refer-

ence materials approved before the meeting that are copied and distributed as supplemental information for a discussion or a laptop for someone with a disability. It's best to have these meeting times set in stone and hold the meetings on a regular schedule (yearly, semiannually, or quarterly). These meetings are what guide an organization or department.

4. *Stand-Up, Information Distribution Meetings.* Sometimes the fastest way to get feedback on an issue is with face-to-face communication. Instead of a long string of e-mails that have to be written and read, it is much more efficient to have all of the members of a team gather together in a small conference room and take a quick vote. Meetings are also great for once-a-week updates so that everyone is quickly informed about the work being done by each member on a team. Everyone who is physically capable should stand for the whole of these meetings (people can get too comfortable in chairs; it's easier to stay on track when you're standing), the meetings should last less than fifteen minutes, and, if there is no printed agenda, the purpose of the meeting should be stated in the first minute of the meeting. Introduction of new staff members, relaying of sensitive information (death of a co-worker, workplace accident, layoffs, or closings of other divisions), and award presentations are good reasons for these information distribution meetings.

Before scheduling any other type of meeting, decide whether it is really necessary and the most productive method for conveying information. If it's well planned and has a rigid time frame, a meeting might be an efficient use of everyone's time. One intense but worthwhile exercise is to consider all the attendees' salaries, determine how much they are paid per minute, and estimate the cost of the meeting to the company. In most cases, the meeting isn't financially worth it—especially if that meeting will be disorganized, irrelevant to its attendees, and/or a poor use of resources. Interviews and sales meetings, however, can definitely be worth the financial investment.

Consider inviting people only to parts of meetings or dismissing them after their portion of the meeting is completed. If you plan your meeting well, you should know at what point in the schedule specific people are needed. Keeping someone in an hour-long meeting when only five minutes are relevant to him is poor planning on your part and a waste of fifty-five minutes of his time.

Participating in Meetings

You might not realize it, but meeting attendees have some control over how quickly a meeting runs and they certainly impact the quality of the discussion.

- *Be prepared.* Read the agenda at least a day in advance of the meeting. Come to the meeting with relevant materials. Have a pen and a pad of paper with you. Turn your BlackBerry to vibrate. Know who else will be at the meeting. Know the goal of the meeting, its location, and its start time. Arrive at the meeting on time.

- *Respect others.* How many times have you been in a meeting where a presenter has had to repeat information because Gary and Stephanie were focusing on their laptops instead of paying attention the first time something was said? Not only does this type of distraction waste Gary's and Stephanie's time, but it also wastes the time of everyone attending the meeting. Focus your attention on who is speaking. Make eye contact. Show that you're listening. Avoid making snide comments to your neighbor. If you're having trouble concentrating, write down in excruciating detail everything the speaker is saying. It will give you something to do, and you can review your detailed notes later if you spaced out on what was being said.

- *Think before you speak.* Before you contribute to a conversation in a meeting, ask yourself: 1) Is this comment helpful and relevant to the topic being discussed right now? (If it's not, save it for after the meeting.) 2) Will this comment be helpful to everyone in the room or just one individual? (If the comment is only helpful to one person, save everyone else's time and talk to that specific person after the meeting.) 3) Can I craft my comment so that it takes less than thirty seconds to express? (If you can't, keep crafting. If you're not presenting, your comments should be brief.)

Planning a Meeting

A well-organized meeting is a thing of beauty. Unfortunately, well-organized meetings are also very rare. If you can learn how to lead efficient and productive meetings, you will have a highly valuable and noticeable skill.

Once you have concluded that you have a reason to have a meeting, your next step is to create a first-rate agenda. All agendas need to be in attendees' hands at least twenty-four hours before the meeting. If you don't know what you're going to discuss a day before the meeting, it's best to cancel and reschedule it when you have a clearer idea.

You should be able to express the meeting's purpose with a one-sentence statement. To develop your purpose statement, finish the following sentence: "At the end of the meeting, attendees will . . ." What comes next in your statement should be concrete, specific, and best achieved through a meeting.

The following is an example of a well-constructed purpose statement:

> At the end of the meeting, attendees will have drafted a one-page annual strategy statement that will guide our team over the next year.

The following is an example of a bad purpose statement:

> At the end of the meeting, attendees will have discussed what is on the agenda.

With the purpose of your meeting defined, you can now work backward to determine how you're going to fulfill your meeting's purpose. To fulfill this purpose, your meeting agenda should have a clear beginning, middle, and end.

Agenda

1. Call meeting to order
    a. State purpose of meeting
    b. Describe how that purpose will be achieved
    c. Relay any information relevant to the remainder
       of the meeting
2. Fulfill the meeting's purpose
3. Conclusion of meeting
    a. Recap all future action items and deadlines that
       were decided during the meeting
    b. State the meeting's fulfilled purpose
    c. Thank everyone for attending the meeting.

After drafting your agenda, make notes for yourself approx-imating how long each section of the agenda should take to complete. The beginning of your meeting might be a minute, the two issues you need to address in the middle of your meet-ing are five minutes each, and the end of your meeting is two minutes. Consider using a stopwatch (better to use one that counts upward so that no buzzer sounds during the meeting) to help keep you on schedule.

When you hold the meeting, stick to the agenda. Don't read the agenda aloud, just move through it in a clear and obvious fashion. If the meeting starts to run off topic, acknowledge the other issue, identify when the remainder of that conversation can take place, and then guide the discussion back to the agenda. It's okay for you to say, "Jason and Dashiell, I like your ideas on XY; can we grab a coffee at two o'clock and discuss it further? I'd like for us to stay on topic right now so that Dana and Kathy can make their ten o'clock meeting with Client Z."

After the meeting and before the start of the next workday, e-mail everyone a list of all the action items and deadlines that were determined during the meeting. This reminder makes it simpler for everyone to record these tasks on their to-do lists.

Phone, Internet, and E-mail Strategies

For all of the positive attributes that come with being constantly connected (being able to make a call in an emergency, texting directions to a friend, etc.), there are a number of downsides, too. Maybe you have a boss who repeatedly calls and leaves messages for you while you're on vacation or maybe you receive more than a hundred spam messages in your e-mail account a day. Technologies that are convenient for you also are convenient to telemarketers, spammers, and people with no respect for your free time. As a result, it's understandable if you have a love-hate relationship with all of your communication devices.

The Phone. When I was in eighth grade, I would talk on the phone every night for a minimum of three hours. I have no specific memories of what my friends and I would discuss for such a ridiculous amount of time, but I'm sure it was world peace and cures for cancer and definitely *not* boys, the latest school gossip, or how cool I thought I was. These days, I average less than two hours on the phone a week. I'm convinced that each person has an allotted amount of phone time in her life, and I used almost all of mine up when I was thirteen.

I go out of my way not to use the phone, especially at work, and I have found this to be a very effective way to stay on task. If someone calls me and leaves a voice mail, I'll send a text message or e-mail in return summarizing what was said in the voice mail and give my response. There is no record of communication with the phone. You don't have anything to reference later and you can't run a search on words used during the conversation. Decisions or instructions can be quickly forgotten. Phones are good for relaying sensitive information to people who aren't physically close to you (like when a coworker in another division leaves for a new job) but bad for transmitting facts and data points.

Since most of us spend time at work dealing with facts and data, the phone should be taking a backseat to other forms of communication. That being said, it's impossible to avoid the phone in the workplace. And there are times when picking up the phone is the best way to handle a situation. The following are suggestions for how to use the phone in an organized way during those times when you need to rely on it:

- *Create talking points.* Before you make a call, jot down notes about what you need to cover in your discussion. This is especially important before conference calls. Like with meetings, you should never make a call without knowing how you want the conversation to end. If you can't construct a purpose statement before dialing, don't dial.

- *Set a timer.* Whenever you call someone, you're interrupting whatever it was the person was doing before you called. Be respectful of this and make the call as brief as possible.

When someone calls you, be up front about how much time you have to be on the phone. Most phone calls should begin as follows: You: "Hello, this is NAME." Caller: "Hello, this is NAME. How are you?" You: "I'm great. I've got X minutes to talk, what can I help you with?" If the person on the other end of the line needs to talk to you for more than the number of minutes you said, then he or she can schedule a block of time to talk with you in the future. You: "Hey, can we talk this afternoon at three? I don't have any afternoon appointments scheduled."

- *Use a headset if you're on the phone for more than half an hour a day.* From an ergonomic perspective, your neck shouldn't be cramped for extended periods of time. Plus, your hands will be free to do mindless tasks while you're on your call—filing papers, putting paper clips away in your drawer, etc. If you're going to be making a lot of noise, though, be sure to hit the mute button so that you don't disrupt the other people on the call.

- *Don't call people and ask whether they received your e-mail.* If you are worried someone didn't receive your initial e-mail, just resend it with a note and the whole content of your previous message. Ask for a confirmation of receipt if you're afraid the e-mails aren't arriving. Not everyone checks their e-mail on your schedule, so don't disrupt them further by calling.

- *Use the do-not-disturb button.* Just because you're sitting at your desk doesn't mean that you have to answer the phone. If you need to concentrate intently on work, hit the do-not-disturb button and let all calls go to voice mail for that period of time. You shouldn't leave the button on all the time, because this practice will reflect poorly on you in the workplace. However, doing it from time to time can significantly improve your productivity.

- *Designate a time to return calls.* I like to return phone calls from twelve thirty to one in the afternoon, after lunch, when my energy level is low. I get a boost from the people I'm talking to, and it's a time when most everyone across the U.S. is at work (twelve thirty PM East Coast time is nine thirty AM on the West Coast).

The Internet. When using the Internet, accept that temptation is everywhere. Set limits to your online behavior. There are some amazing tools on the Internet that can allow you to accomplish productive work, but this doesn't override the fact that the Internet also acts as an alluring siren eager to distract you from your goals. Avoid the time-wasting elements and focus instead on those that will help you to be more productive.

Set up an online collaboration system so you and your co-workers can freely communicate with one another throughout the day. Programs like Campfire (campfirenow.com) provide a platform where team members can talk to one another without having to pick up a phone, chat over Instant Messenger, or type a more formal e-mail. The system also logs conversations so that they can be searched at a later time. If you're away from the office for a few days, you can go back and see what was discussed in your absence. These systems are great for clarifying details and brainstorming.

Skype (skype.com) is a way to video chat in an inexpensive and humanized way. Use a webcam with the program so that you can have a virtual face-to-face conversation. Being able to see facial expressions and other nonverbal cues in addition to what you hear increases your level of understanding about what is being communicated. You can also record your video chat. There are numerous third-party Skype recorder programs for both the Mac and PC; just be sure to let the person you're talking to know that you're recording the conversation. Apply the same guidelines we established for the phone to ensure that you're using the program efficiently.

If you're reading the newspaper every day or following any blogs, use an RSS feed reader to have that information pushed to you. RSS stands for "Really Simple Syndication." An RSS feed reader captures content from blogs and news services and lists these articles in your feed reader's inbox. Programs like Google Reader, NewsGator, Ensembli, Bloglines, and others give you varying levels of control on how you access your RSS feeds. If you want to tailor a feed to provide only certain kinds of content to your feed reader, you can make this happen with a program called Yahoo! Pipes (pipes.yahoo.com).

If you're working on a deadline, hide your browser's icon so that you're not tempted to jump online out of habit. Again, use a timer to prevent time from slipping away from you. If you have fifteen minutes to read your favorite sites over your lunch break, make sure that fifteen minutes doesn't turn into two hours. When organizing your RSS feeds, group them by priority instead of content and work your way through your list by reading the most important feeds first. And feel welcome to declare

RSS feed reader bankruptcy at any time. Mark all the posts as read and start again fresh.

E-mail. When used effectively, e-mail can help you to be more productive in less time. Unfortunately, though, most of us are overwhelmed by the amount of e-mail we receive in our workplace inboxes. Eight hours at work can easily include a hundred e-mail messages from colleagues and clients. Managing this avalanche of communication can be a full-time job if you don't take the steps to get the situation under control.

- *Cure your e-mail addiction.* The first step to managing your e-mail is accepting that the majority of items in your inbox do not contain life-or-death information. I always hear the excuse, "Things are different in my office, I have to check my e-mails the minute they arrive in my inbox." Okay, maybe things are different in your office, but every person I've coached has eventually admitted that they won't get fired if they only check e-mail twice an hour. And most of these people eventually only check e-mail at the top of each hour or even less frequently in a day.

- *Kill the notifications.* Go into your e-mail program's settings and turn off the new e-mail notification icon or sound so that it's not tempting you to click on it. Then only check your e-mail at nine AM, eleven AM, two PM, and five PM each workday (or whatever set schedule works best for you).

- *The fewer you send, the fewer you will receive.* We all have to generate e-mails, but that doesn't mean we have to generate an endless stream of them. Find alternate ways to talk to your clients and coworkers with project management and group collaboration tools. Communicate new offerings to clients over a company blog or through social media instead of relying on e-mail as your only outreach method.

- *Make it short and sweet.* Productivity experts encourage limiting messages to no more than three sentences or seven sentences. I think these are good rules for most of your e-mails, but you can also waste time trying to craft what you need to say into such a specific, itty-bitty package. Instead of spending time counting sentences, just remember that people tend to mimic the style of your message in their response. If you send a short e-mail, chances are you'll receive a brief e-mail in return. Kevin Rose, the brain behind digg.com, is rumored to write "Sent from mobile phone" at the bottom of all of his e-mails, even ones not sent from his mobile phone. This way, when people send him long e-mails, he doesn't seem rude when he only sends back a short response.

- *Keep it out of the news.* Before you send any e-mail, ask yourself how you would feel if the content of your message ended up on the front page of a national newspaper. There is no such thing as e-mail privacy. Hackers break into accounts, your network administrator probably already reads your messages, and once you hit the send button you have no control over what the person who receives it will do with the message. Office politics, top secret company information, snide comments about clients or coworkers, and anything that could come back to bite you should never be in an e-mail. The good news is, if you're in the habit of sending e-mails like this, you'll notice an immediate decrease in the amount of e-mail passing through your system.

Beyond these simple tactics that can be easily applied to just about everyone's inbox, the best e-mail management system is different for everyone. That being said, e-mails that arrive in our inboxes typically fall into one of four categories: *spam, FYI, instant action possible,* and *delayed action needed.*

- *Spam.* This is actually the easiest e-mail to handle. You just delete it. Once you determine that a message is spam, it can go away forever. Also, install a heavy-duty spam filter on your system so as little spam as possible gets through in the first place.

- *FYI.* These e-mails contain things you need to know but don't require you to do anything with the information once you've read it. If the e-mail is short, you can read it and be done with it. If it's long, like a journal article or a company-wide memo, you might not have the time to read the message and make sense of it. At the point you realize that you can't read the entire e-mail, it transforms from an *FYI* e-mail into a *delayed action needed* e-mail (see page 136).

- *Instant action possible.* These e-mails are usually easy to deal with since you can immediately respond to them and be done: "What day is the project due?" "November 3." You can kick out a response in less than fifteen seconds and move on to the next message. These rarely cause inbox clutter. I wish all e-mails were like this. "May I buy you a new car?" "Yes, please."

- *Delayed action needed.* These e-mails are the root cause of most e-mail management problems. They require that something be done, but that something can't happen right now. You need to find a way to handle these bad boys if you're ever going to get your e-mail situation under control. Review your old e-mails and identify any patterns of actions these messages usually require. Do you need to schedule appointments, confirm information with someone else, or perform a search in a database? If you can find patterns like this in your e-mails, it will help you to establish routines and processes for handling this work.

Think of each *delayed action needed* e-mail as a different work assignment, and treat it in the same manner as you do all other requests for your time. Imagine that the person who sent you the e-mail is standing in your office asking you to do something. What would you do with that request? Would you write it on a to-do list? Schedule it on your calendar? Create an action item in a project management program? You wouldn't just leave the person waiting for an answer. Whatever you would do for an in-person request, do exactly that for the *delayed action needed* e-mail request. Once you have taken the proper action, you can immediately move the e-mail out of your inbox and into another folder.

I have three folders in addition to my inbox in my e-mail program. The largest folder is "Archive," where all messages go after I schedule the work on my calendar or in my project management system. I save all e-mails in my "Archive" folder so that if I have any questions about what someone sent to me, I can do a search and reference the original. The second folder I have is "Ask Unclutterer." Readers send in questions, and we answer them every Friday in a column that is suitably named Ask Unclutterer. This folder is where I store these questions until I use them in the column, and then I move them to the "Archive" folder. The third folder I have is named "Read Me." This is where I put long e-mails that require reading but that I don't have time to read the minute I receive them in my inbox. Before I put an e-mail in this folder, I make sure that it doesn't ask that I do anything else beyond reading it and I also put a task on my to-do list that says something like "Read memo from Angela on the Client X matter by Tuesday afternoon. E-mail is in 'Read Me' folder." I have built fifteen minutes into my daily routine after my lunch phone calls to read all the items in this folder. Once I've read the e-mails, I move them to my "Archive" folder.

Whatever system you implement, apply the same rules to e-mail that you do for your other work. Like I mentioned earlier, when someone comes into your office asking you to do something, you don't ask him to hang out in your office for a few days until you choose to do what he wants you to do. Instead, you immediately input his request into your to-do system and then he leaves your office.

Additional E-mail Tips

- When e-mailing groups of people with a message that isn't part of an ongoing conversation, blind copy the recipients to avoid an accidental "reply all" situation.
- Create preset e-mail groups in your digital address book: board of directors, team leaders, team members, committee members, executive assistants, etc. Instead of manually entering everyone's address and possibly forgetting someone, you simply type the group name into the "To:" field. All e-mail addresses for that group are inserted automatically.
- Pick up the telephone or jump on Skype at the first indication that an e-mail message has been misinterpreted.
- Respect the subject line. Be detailed in your subject lines, and don't change subject lines in e-mail conversations on the same topic. That being said, if you have a point on a new topic, start a new e-mail conversation with a new subject line and keep the conversations separate. This helps people to sort through their e-mail and helps them to keep from missing important information that could get buried in a conversation thread.

Powerful Presentations

Staying awake is a Herculean task in a dark room while a presenter reads a speech word-for-word in a monotone voice from a series of text slides on a PowerPoint presentation. I've nodded off to sleep on more than one occasion when I've been in these situations. The only thing that impresses me about these dismal presentations is that the speakers manage to stay awake. I don't know how they do it.

You don't have to be a world-class public speaker to make a good presentation; you just need to be prepared and organized. Similar to how you created the agenda for your meeting, determine what you want your audience to know by the end of your presentation. Complete the sentence "At the end of my presentation, audience members will . . ." Be sure to voice this goal at the start of your presentation so that your audience knows why you're speaking. Once you all know where you're heading, you can focus on how to get there. Being organized also helps reduce the nervousness you might be feeling about speaking in front of others.

When you're crafting the body of your presentation, remember your favorite teacher. What methods did he use that helped you learn? Did he drone on in darkness behind a slew of PowerPoint slides? Probably not. Your favorite teacher likely used a combination of animated lectures, hands-on activities, independent analyses, and readings to help you learn. Your presentation should include those same visual, auditory, active, and independent elements. Interest people's eyes, ears, body, and mind in what you're doing. Interact with your audience in a way that shows you sincerely care that they leave your presentation knowing more than they did when they arrived. Since you know that people process information in different ways (remember what was discussed on Monday in the closet organizing section), you want to be sure to engage every member of your audience.

✓ Do use slides in your presentation if they illustrate elements that are better explained with the help of a visual aid.

✓ Do use charts and graphs to display quantitative information.

✓ Do bring in physical examples that audience members can hold and inspect if you're talking about a product.

✓ Do enroll in a speech class for business professionals if you haven't made a presentation in the last two years, or join Toastmasters (toastmasters.org).

✓ Do create concise and valuable presentations, and practice the whole of your presentation at least twice before giving it to a group.

✓ Do have an outline of what you need to say and how much time you can spend on each section.

✓ Do get out from behind the podium and engage your audience.

✗ Don't write out every word of your presentation. You want to be comfortable and speak naturally to your audience, not at them.

✗ Don't use text-only slides.

✗ Don't use gimmicky features that distract from your message. Slides shouldn't dissolve or fly in from one side of the screen, and nothing on the screen should dance or blink.

Selectively Saying Yes

Being a good communicator improves your productivity and the overall quality of your work. One of the most advanced communication skills is learning how to say no to someone without damaging your relationship with that person. The truth of the matter is that you cannot say yes to every request that comes your way because you will become overworked and dissatisfied with your job, and ultimately the work you're hired to do will suffer. It is important to be a team player, but it's also important to fulfill your primary obligations.

If you have spent your entire work life saying yes to every request that has come your way, you will undoubtedly feel guilty the first time you don't agree to handle a request. You'll feel like you let someone down or that the project will fail if you aren't a part of the team. It's okay if you feel this way. But over time, you'll start to see that others respect the improved quality in your work and will come to appreciate your selective nature. Also, remember that you do have to say yes from time to time, so you won't continually be saying no to everything that comes your way.

When deciding whether to say no or yes, begin by writing out your job priorities. This list should reflect your job description and the goals you set with your manager during your yearly review. It should be a short list—fewer than ten items—and should only include those things that you are certain you will get fired or lose your clients over if you don't complete them. These priorities make up your "yes" list. These are the things you will agree to do no matter what. If anyone asks you to do anything related to these items, you will be a team player and jump right in with both feet.

This list also acts as your "no" filter. When someone makes a request for your time that isn't related to any of the items on your priority list, you need to say no and decline the request. (There are a few times when you will have to say yes to nonpriority items because your job depends on it, but these times will hopefully be few and far between.)

There is an art to saying no in such a way that you don't come off as being abrasive or difficult. It might make sense for you to practice with friends who work for different organizations. (And it will help put things in perspective when your friends say, "They asked you to do *what*?") You may feel silly at first, but practicing will help you sound more natural when you need to use the skill in your workplace. The list below shows examples of ways that you can diplomatically say no without being a Negative Nelly:

- "I think you have a great idea, but I don't think I'm the best person to help you on that matter. Have you talked to Margaret? I think she might be interested in working on something like this. I'll introduce the two of you."

- "I'm working with Teri on the Client X matter for our meeting first thing Friday morning. After I file my report, I should have some more time on my schedule. If you can wait until Monday, I will be able to help you. If you need the work completed before then, I unfortunately can't help."

- "Paul, I am grateful that you thought of me, but my schedule is full until the end of the month. Can I e-mail you the names and e-mail addresses of some of my coworkers who might be available?"

- "Mr. Johnston, I'm starting to feel overwhelmed by all of the requests that have recently been asked of me. Can we meet after lunch for ten minutes? I would appreciate your guidance on how I should best prioritize my time."

- "My team is currently working on X, Y, and Z, which are all due for client review in the next three weeks. Our biggest priority right now is meeting these deadlines and we've put all other assignments on hold until these three goals are met. I would love to talk with you about your idea further, but that conversation and any decisions about that project will have to wait."

When you say no to a request, try to:

1. Treat the request being made of you with respect. Just because you don't have time for it doesn't mean it doesn't have merit.
2. Express appreciation for the fact that the person thought you would be qualified to fulfill the request.
3. Communicate any alternatives, such as a different date or another person who may be able to help instead.
4. Don't leave room for negotiation. State the facts and be firm in your speech.

Wednesday Evening:
Your Kitchen and Dining Room

The kitchen and dining room are the heart of the home. This is where you create and enjoy the meals that give you energy to do all the things you want to do. Healthy eating is as important to work-life symbiosis as sleep. When the kitchen and dining room are chaotic, you eat food that isn't very healthy, worry about dinner plans, and are irritated that your schedule has been disrupted. When the kitchen and dining room function like a well-oiled machine, however, you have less stress, eat well, and enjoy sharing a meal at home. When these spaces and their activities are organized, you never wonder what you'll have for dinner or if you have the right ingredients to make what you want.

Working the Room

Before you pull any food out of your pantry or start putting together your next grocery list, walk into your kitchen and take a long look at it. What do you see? Are there dirty dishes or small appliances on the counter? Where are your trash can and recycling bins? Do the major appliances work well? Are you missing any cupboard doors or drawer pulls? How is the condition of your floor?

If a kitchen is going to be the heart of your home, it needs to:

1. Be a sanitary and safe environment.

2. Have hands-free, easy access to a centrally located trash can.

3. Be a place where you enjoy spending time.

What work will it take to meet these three requirements?

The first requirement for a sanitary and safe environment is nonnegotiable. If you have ants, roaches, silverfish, flour beetles, mice, mold, mildew, or rotting food anywhere in your kitchen, you have to take care of these problems now. You cannot store or serve food in a hazardous environment. If you need to, call a professional exterminator or a mold removal service and follow their directions for making your kitchen sanitary.

Additionally, every aspect of your kitchen needs to be as safe as it possibly can. Have electric and gas appliances serviced if necessary, hire a plumber to inspect your water lines into the sink, dishwasher, and refrigerator (if you have an ice maker), and have a carpenter inspect shelving, counters, and cabinetry if any of these areas aren't in their best condition. Your floors should be free of obstructions of all kinds and in superior condition. If you have owned your food preparation knives for many years, take them to be professionally sharpened. Dull knives are dangerous and increase your risk of injury.

Having hands-free, easy access to a centrally located trash can is the second requirement. The trash can is the most essential piece of equipment in your kitchen; you use it every time you cook. If you store your trash can under your sink or in a pantry, remove it from the cabinet during meal preparation and place it where it is most convenient for your work. It's unsanitary and inefficient to touch a cabinet pull or doorknob with dirty and full hands. A poorly placed trash can doesn't help you in the kitchen; it hinders you. The best trash cans open with a foot lever, have lids that open out away from the trash (instead of swinging in toward the trash), and have a mechanism to secure the top edge of your trash bag. This way, you can access the trash can with full hands, you don't have to constantly clean trash off of the lid, and you can grab the top of the bag to tie it up when the bag gets full.

Third, your kitchen should be a place where you enjoy spending time. A clean, organized, well-lit, and safe kitchen can go a long way toward making you want to spend time there. Spruce up the room to make it a welcoming environment. Beyond the stuff, is there anything you dislike about your kitchen? Do you need better task lighting? Do the walls need a new coat of paint? Look at the room and determine whether there are changes that could make it more inviting.

After you've answered the questions at the start of this section and met the three essential requirements, pull out all of the food from your pantry and clear your kitchen cabinets, shelves, countertops, and drawers of small appliances, tableware, pots, pans, and whatever else you have. Temporarily store these items on your dining room table so that you can get a complete idea of everything you own. As you put items onto the table, group them by function and purpose. Put like items with like items (spices with spices, grains with grains). Similar to when you laid out all your clothes on your bed, prepare to be amazed by the amount of things you have been storing in your kitchen.

Later, when it comes time to return items to the kitchen, put things where you use them. Pots, pans, and potholders should be kept near the stove. Store coffee mugs in a cupboard near your coffeemaker. Keep silverware in a drawer near the cupboard that holds your plates. Put items you don't use regularly in the highest and lowest sections of your storage. Items you use every day should be stored at hip and shoulder height. Make your kitchen as intuitive, sanitary, and efficient as possible.

Unitaskers

On Unclutterer.com, we have a weekly feature called "Unitasker Wednesday," where we like to make fun of single-use items that manage to make their way into our homes. We joke about them to remind us that organizing doesn't have to be overly serious. I'm mentioning them in the kitchen section because so many unitaskers are made for food preparation—a spoon made only for avocado scooping, a monogrammed branding iron for your steaks, goggles to wear only when chopping onions.

We first heard Alton Brown use the word *unitasker* on an episode of *Good Eats*. Some unitaskers are essential (a fire extinguisher, for example), but it's better to have well-made multitaskers when possible. Small appliances and utensils that only perform one specific task can easily become clutter in your kitchen (like a fork made for the sole purpose of getting pickles out of a jar!). If you put a single-use item to work every day, then that item has high utility and doesn't meet the definition of a unitasker. The item has to be of no use to *you* for it to meet the definition. In my kitchen, cookie cutters are unitaskers because I rarely bake cookies. I have a circular biscuit cutter that I use once a month on biscuits and scones that can also be used to make round cookie shapes for the once-in-a-decade time I decide to make cookies. In a pastry chef's kitchen, though, cookie cutters might be used so often that they have to be replaced on an annual basis. One person's unitasker is another person's kitchen staple.

When it comes time to return items to your kitchen, get rid of all of your unitaskers. Any single-use items you haven't used in the last year definitely need to go. Only keep things you use, not things you might one day use. Donate unwanted items to charity, sell them on eBay, list them on Freecycle, or give them to a friend—do whatever you need to do, just get them out of your kitchen.

Unclutterer.com reader Alex Fayle passed along a helpful suggestion for determining what you actually use and don't use in your kitchen. "A simple way of knowing if you actually use things is to get removable colored dots and stick one to each of your small appliances and kitchen gadgets. As you use your things, take off the dot (hence why you want to get removable dots)." After six months, get rid of all of the things that still have dots.

Tools of the Trade

As you start returning objects to your kitchen, make sure to group objects with similar items like you did when you were organizing your bathroom. Use silverware trays, drawer dividers, and containers so that items don't get lost. If you don't already own drawer dividers, buy ones that are dishwasher safe to make cleaning them simple. Get rid of any damaged utensils and only replace these items as necessary. Organizing these drawers makes it simple to quickly find what you're looking for when you're cooking.

When you move on to cooking and baking items, be sure to store these properly to protect them from being damaged. Don't stack anything more than three deep (you don't want to warp your pans) and use store-bought products to organize your lids and baking sheets. Also, arrange items so they are easily accessible and simple to store again after cleaning. If a storage system is difficult to maintain, it won't stay organized.

Plastic storage items (like Tupperware and Rubbermaid products) and other food storage materials can quickly clutter up your cabinets if you're not careful. Recycle any items that are stained or damaged. Many manufacturers of these products also make organizers to keep these objects from creating a mess in your cupboards, and I highly recommend buying them or making something similar to keep these objects contained. A worthwhile exercise is to pretend that you have food in each of the storage containers and try to see how many of them you can stuff into your refrigerator and freezer. Think of it like a game of refrigerator Tetris. When your refrigerator and freezer are completely full, you have reached the maximum amount of food storage containers you could ever use at once. Get rid of anything that didn't fit since you know you could never have a need for it.

Play a similar game with your serving dishes. Set your table with plates and glasses, and then fill the rest of the area with serving dishes, trays, and bowls. Whatever doesn't fit on your table can't possibly be used for a dinner party. Sell or donate the extras to charity and free up space in your cupboards.

The only items that should be stored on your countertops are those things that you use every day or every time you use the kitchen. Dust and grime will collect on anything left on the counter. Think of your kitchen counters the same way you did your desk at work. We had a bread box for a couple of years and eventually got rid of it when we started calling it the "rotten box." We would put bread in it and then forget we had bread inside of it. No need to waste valuable counter space on items you don't use.

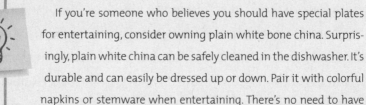

If you're someone who believes you should have special plates for entertaining, consider owning plain white bone china. Surprisingly, plain white china can be safely cleaned in the dishwasher. It's durable and can easily be dressed up or down. Pair it with colorful napkins or stemware when entertaining. There's no need to have two sets of dishes with one set as convenient and versatile as these.

Not having anything on the countertops also applies to dirty dishes. After a meal or snack, food service and preparation items need to be immediately cleaned or loaded into the dishwasher.

If you have a dishwasher, run it every night after dinner and unload it every morning before breakfast. (If you live alone or just have one roommate, you may be able to run it every other night or every third night after dinner.) Running the dishwasher on a set schedule will alleviate the stress of keeping your kitchen clean. If you don't have a dishwasher, wash your dishes after every meal and snack, no exceptions. Any dirty plate, bowl, or glass on your counter is an open invitation to bugs, pests, and mold.

Cleaning Out the Pantry and Refrigerator

When you finish returning all nonfood items to your kitchen, it's time to tackle the contents of your pantry. First, make sure that no food items are expired. If you have no memory of buying an item and you can't find its expiration date on its container, don't take the risk. Toss it.

Next, get rid of any food that has passed its prime. People might tell you foods like spices are good for many years after their labels say, which, to some extent, may be true. However, expiration dates aren't always about the food. Water doesn't expire, but bottled water has an expiration date on it because the plastic container decomposes and leaches chemicals into the water after a certain period of time. The expiration on the bottle identifies the point when the chemicals from the bottle may start to interact with the water and create a poison. Spices stored in plastic containers run the same risk. So it's best to follow the manufacturer's suggestions.

The website Still Tasty (stilltasty.com) is also a terrific resource for determining whether a food is safe to eat. Pull up the site, enter a food into the search bar, and learn whether you should keep or get rid of it. This is especially useful for determining whether foods stored in a freezer are okay. I like to keep a permanent marker in my cupboard to write the purchase date and open date on the lids and packaging of food containers. I also keep a roll of masking tape in my pantry so that I can make labels for this information on reusable containers. These purchase and open dates make it immediately apparent if something is good to eat.

When you return items to your pantry, consider using tiered platforms at the back of shelves so that items don't get lost and forgotten. Use baskets and bins to group like items together. (Baskets are especially great for breakfast items like cereal, so you only have to pull out a single basket each morning to set on the table.) Store drink mixes and spice packets in an index card file. Save space by storing soup cans in a soda can rack. Make sure you can reach everything in your pantry.

Repeat the whole process of clearing out your pantry and checking expiration dates every six months, in addition to throwing out expired items as you find them through regular use. If you spot an item that is nearing its expiration date, find a recipe that uses the ingredient and commit to making the dish and eating it in the next week.

Now is also a good time to clean out your refrigerator and freezer. Check for expiration dates on packaged foods, get rid of anything moldy, freezer burned, or rotten, and wipe down shelves and seals with a wet cloth and a mild detergent. Get into the habit of clearing clutter from your refrigerator and freezer before your weekly trip to the grocery store.

Cookbooks and Recipes

If you can afford to sacrifice the space, devote at least one cupboard shelf to cookbook storage in your kitchen. If you have a large collection of cookbooks, start by sorting them into three piles: books you use once a week, books you use once a month, and books you rarely or never open. Any book you use once a week should immediately go on your bookshelf—it's a trusted companion. Any book you rarely or never open should immediately be donated to your local library or sold to a used bookstore.

Books that you use once a month or on a semiregular basis are more difficult to process. Separate these books into piles based on type and occasion: baking, slow cooking, general, grilling/barbecue, Thai, desserts, French, etc. Get rid of any book that is inferior to the others in its category. Can you store all of the remaining books on your shelf? If not, try a third round of sorting. This time, separate the books into two piles: books with more than five recipes you like, and books with fewer than five recipes you like. For books with fewer than five recipes, simply copy down the recipes you like and get rid of the books. By this point, your cookbook collection should be small enough to be contained on a single shelf.

For single recipe cards and recipes you print from the Internet, store these in a recipe notebook:

What you'll need:

- ☐ A vinyl-coated three-ring notebook with a front pocket
- ☐ Sticky notes (I prefer two sizes—one larger, one smaller)
- ☐ A pen that dries quickly and doesn't streak
- ☐ A pack of fifty sheet protectors (or as many as necessary)
- ☐ Ten notebook tab dividers (or as many as necessary)
- ☐ Ten or more sheets of looseleaf notebook paper

Assembly:

- ☐ Make a cover and artwork for the spine of the notebook, so that it is clearly identified as your treasured recipes.

- ☐ Put the sticky notes and pen in the front pocket of the notebook. You'll want these easily accessible for when you make notes on the recipes ("Too much salt"/"Add five minutes to baking time"/"Mom's favorite"). Also, if it's a recipe that I make often, I'll write the ingredients on a sticky note, move it from the recipe to my weekly shopping list, and then move it back to the recipe when I return home.

- ☐ Drop in the looseleaf paper so that it will sit at the back of the notebook. This paper is for you to write down your own recipes as you invent them in the kitchen.

- ☐ Write the following categories on the tabs of the dividers: *Appetizers, Salads, Soups, Breads, Beef Entrees, Pork Entrees,*

Chicken Entrees, Vegetarian Entrees, Other Entrees, and *Desserts.* If you have other categories, add those accordingly.

☐ Put your recipes into the sheet protectors, and then organize them by categorical tab. You can put in one recipe per sheet protector, or you can put two recipes in each back-to-back.

☐ Load up your notebook and enjoy having all of your recipes in one location.

Coupon clippers can make a similar notebook for coupons. Set up categories based on the organization of your grocery store and be sure to pull out all the expired coupons once a week.

If you have a computer installed in your kitchen, you might want to consider a digital recipe system for your collection, like eChef software. I don't recommend bringing a laptop into the kitchen if it's not protected to use around food because of spills and messes that can permanently damage your computer.

Meal Planning and Eliminating Mealtime Stress

How many times a week do you find yourself saying, "I'm starving, let's see what is in the kitchen" or "What should I make for dinner?" A weekly meal plan alleviates the stress that comes along with deciding what to do for dinner and makes it easy to create a nutritious meal at home. When you're organized, you know the ingredients you need are in the kitchen, what you'll eat, and how long it should take you to make the meal, and you'll be able to estimate your amount of cleanup.

On page 157, I've included a sample of the worksheet I use for meal planning. Schedule half an hour each week to plan meals for the coming week. You'll need a copy of the worksheet, a stack of cookbooks, and sticky notes. Flip through your favorite cookbooks and recipe notebook, flagging the recipes you want to use for the week. If you're a coupon user, match coupons with recipes so that you can take advantage of that week's deals.

Next, put an "X" on the worksheet through any of the meals that you know will be eaten out of the house for friends' birthdays or whatever is lined up on your calendar. Then match up recipes you've marked in the cookbooks with openings on the schedule. If any of the items need preparation hours or days beforehand, list those under the "Prep for Tomorrow" section to help with managing your time. (For example, the dough I make for homemade pizza crusts needs to be made twenty-four hours in advance. So if I want pizza tomorrow, I have to make the dough today.) Also, having at least two snacks listed on the worksheet ensures that you have healthy snack choices available in your pantry.

When matching recipes with meals, review the recipe and write down any ingredients on the grocery list section of the worksheet. This helps you plan what you need from the store and/or farmer's market. Once your ingredient list is complete, look through your pantry and cross off any items from your list that you already have.

You also can create a similar meal-planning worksheet in a spreadsheet program (like Excel) on your computer and complete the whole process digitally if it is more convenient for you. Tape the finished meal plan to the inside of a cabinet door so that you can refer to it throughout the week.

	Breakfast	Lunch	Dinner	Snacks (2)	Prep for Tomorrow	Grocery List
Sunday						
Monday						
Tuesday						
Wednesday						
Thursday						
Friday						
Saturday						
Key/Notes:						

Shopping as Sport

The next time you're at the grocery store, ask the clerk at the customer service desk whether he or she has a map of the store. Most chain grocery stores have these available for customers. If your store doesn't have printed maps, walk around the store and draw yourself a quick diagram. From this point forward, use this map as a guide for structuring your shopping lists. My lists always begin with fruits and vegetables because it is the first section I encounter in the grocery store. Organize your list based on the fastest route through the store to eliminate the chances that you'll forget an item and have to backtrack.

If your grocery store is open twenty-four hours a day, take advantage of the off-peak hours when the store is empty and the clerks are more willing to talk and answer questions. The markets are packed on weekends, which adds time to the chore. My husband and I like to each grab a cart, split the list in half, and race each other to see who can finish first. I like to go on Tuesday nights when the store is pretty empty and I'm already out running other errands.

Your Dining Room

You've spent time uncluttering your kitchen, preparing your meal plan and grocery list, and speeding through your shopping. Now is the time to reap the benefits of your work. Treat yourself to a sit-down meal at your dining room table.

Clear the clutter off, under, and around your table. Get rid of unused items and things that don't belong in the dining room. If you have a buffet or sideboard in your dining room, pull everything out of it and sort through it the same way you did with your kitchen cabinets. When you put back the useful items, group like items together and don't keep more than you can store.

Sure, from time to time you might temporarily turn your table into a homework station or a craft bench, but you should make a commitment to having it open for every meal. There is something relaxing about setting a place at the table and eating a plated meal—especially in the middle of a busy week. If you have roommates or a family, meals are a nice time to talk about the day's events and share in one another's lives. The dining room should be a place that connects you to food, family, and friends.

chapter 5

Thursday

It's Thursday and your newly uncluttered closet, entryway, bathroom, bedroom, kitchen, and chore routines are already making your home a more serene place to live. At work, you've organized your desk, office, files, and communication processes. You have accomplished a great deal and you should take delight in your success. Regardless of how quickly you moved through the process or how much practice it has taken you to acquire these new skills, all routes still lead to the same place—a remarkable life.

Today's plan includes organizing your living spaces, gaining control of projects and workflow like a time-management expert, and bringing order to your home office. The finish line is on the horizon, and uncluttering these three areas of your life will help you make significant progress toward work-life symbiosis. Keep your focus on what matters most and enjoy the benefits from the clutter you've already cleared; the next few days of work are about to fly by.

Thursday Morning: Your Living Spaces

For most of us, living rooms serve multiple purposes. In my home, the living room serves as the guest bedroom (we have a pullout couch in the middle of the room), a reading room (two walls are lined with bright orange bookcases), a music room (we have two guitars, a mandolin, a violin, a pedal steel guitar, two amplifiers, and a music stand), and a place for people to hang out. Yours might also be a playroom, game room, and television room. Your home may even have many living rooms. One commonality among all of these purposes and spaces, however, is that they are where you do a lot of living. And living, inevitably, stirs up clutter.

Finding Space for Living

As you have done in the other rooms of your home, start this uncluttering project by first defining the purpose(s) of the room(s) and then clearing the clutter. By now, these two steps should be familiar to you. How do you use this room? What objects need to live in this space and what objects don't?

I like to grab a laundry basket and walk through the room gathering everything that doesn't belong—shoes, jackets, old newspapers, an abandoned coffee mug. When the basket is full, sort through its contents and get rid of the clutter. Any items that should be stored in other rooms should be returned, and set on the couch any wayward objects that need to remain in the living room but don't yet have a permanent home. You may need to fill up the laundry basket more than once, or even a few dozen times; just keep filling the basket and sorting through it until all of the clutter is gone from the room.

Once you are left with only the things that should be in this room, you need to find storage space for the objects that you set on the couch and your other things. Do you have sturdy bookshelves for your books? A magazine rack or appropriate storage solution for your periodicals? A place to store board games, video games, DVDs, and/or CDs? Is there a nest of cables poking out from behind your entertainment center? Do you have an entertainment center? What you do in your living room determines what kind of storage you need to contain related objects.

Storage Ideas for Your Living Room

- Closets in or near the living room can be outfitted with shelving (like Elfa shelves) to store games and craft projects.

- Have boxes, baskets, and bins for loose items so that it is obvious where things should live.

- Store like items with like items, so that you can pull out one bin that has all the objects you'll need to do a specific task.

- Try not to stack containers and boxes more than three high so that objects are easy to get to and return after using.

- Attach large hooks to the back wall of your closet to hang up messy vacuum hoses.

- Use end tables with drawers to store magazines and remote controls.

- Make it a habit to only have one issue of a magazine in your home at a time. When the new *Popular Science* arrives, immediately recycle last month's *Popular Science* regardless of whether you read it. If you haven't found time in four weeks to read the print version, you're not going to find time in the next four weeks to read two issues.

- Think about multiuse items when buying new objects for this space, like ottomans with interior storage.

- Store CDs and DVDs in notebooks or digitize your collection so that you aren't overwhelmed with cases.

- Consider subscribing to Netflix or using On Demand and streaming movies into your home when you want to watch them and getting rid of your DVDs entirely.

If you're someone with decorative knickknacks, now is the time to evaluate whether you really need or want each object. Does looking at it make you happy? Does it reflect the remarkable life you want to lead? Refer back to the questions for things already in your home that were listed in the Foundations chapter. Does the knickknack warrant the answer "yes" to every one of the questions? If not, it's time to get rid of the object. Remember, the less you own, the less you have to clean.

Displaying Collections

Parents often write to me and ask what they should do with all of their child's art projects and graded papers. My suggestion is to create a gallery space in your home for the most treasured items. If you don't have children, these suggestions also apply to any collection you might have—high-end fountain pens, action figures, antique kitchen gadgets. Whatever the collection, you should focus on quality items instead of quantity. Keep the best and get rid of the rest.

For school projects, temporarily display the work of that semester on a single shelf. At the end of every semester, lay out all of the good papers and artwork on the dining room table. Talk with your child about the past semester and about the collection of objects on the table. Then ask him to pick one assignment and one piece of artwork that he likes the best. Whatever he chooses will become part of the "permanent gallery." These two items can be kept, and everything else can be digitally photographed and removed from the house.

If it's another type of collection, go through it in a similar manner. Set the whole of your collection out on your dining room table. Choose the best pieces to keep, the ones that are in the finest condition and mean the most to you, and get rid of the rest. The whole of your collection should be on display. If you really value the items, then you shouldn't store them in boxes out of sight in a damp basement or drafty attic. The amount of display space you have will likely determine how many objects you can keep. Also, if you add to the collection in the future, be prepared to get rid of one of the items in your current collection. Your home is a place to live, not a museum.

Once the collection is a manageable size, set up a permanent gallery in your house to display it. We use an art gallery system in our home to display our collection of my father's photographs.[8] There is a track at the top of the wall and cables hang from the track. There are hooks on the cables to hang artwork. The best part about the art gallery system is that you can slide the cables and hooks wherever you want along the track without having to put any nails into the wall. You can easily hang shelves next to the cables for three-dimensional items.

A child's gallery instantly gives him a conversation topic he can have with other people who come into your home, and it shows him that the work he does at school is valued at home. It keeps clutter to a minimum and your kid can have an active role in making decisions. If the gallery is for your personal collection, it shows that you truly value these items and lets visitors to your home share in the joy you get from collecting these objects.

Slimming Down Your Bookshelves

Since you're reading this book, I'm going to make the wild assumption that you read. People who read also typically have problems with overflowing bookshelves. You can't stop at just one book.

Apply the same philosophy to uncluttering your bookshelves that you did to your wardrobe collection: You cannot keep more books than you have space on your bookshelves to store. If you have more books than shelf space, you will always have books cluttering up your living spaces.

But cutting down on the amount of physical books that you own does not mean that you have to get rid of the great information inside of your books. On Wednesday, I presented one strategy for curbing bookshelf clutter, and that was to access literature as audiobooks and ebooks. Digital files take up significantly less space than shelves of books, and it's easy to take them with you. If you have a book in both paper and digital formats, it's time to release the paper version out into the world.

For the books that remain on your shelves, here are some hard and fast rules to apply:

- Give away any books that you don't plan on reading or referencing again, are in the public domain, and can be found in their entirety online.

- Keep the leather-bound copy of *The Scarlet Letter* that your grandmother gave you on her deathbed.

- Give away or recycle out-of-date reference books. They're full of inaccurate data.

- Keep books that you love and books that provide you with significant utility.

- Give away books that you've been storing for the sole purpose of impressing your houseguests. If you've never read the complete works of Shakespeare, and you never plan to read the complete works of Shakespeare, get rid of the complete works of Shakespeare.

Once you have purged all of the books from your home that don't meet these guidelines, think about organizing your books in a way that makes the greatest sense to you: Invent your own cataloging system, use the Dewey Decimal or Library of Congress method, alphabetize by author last name, or loosely cluster them by subject. Since the books that are left in your collection are ones that you have use for or derive information from, you should be able to find them on your shelves when you need them.

Maintaining Order in Your Living Room

Once the clutter is gone from your living room and everything has a storage solution, make a commitment to keeping your living room orderly. Similar to the advice I gave when I was talking about your desk at work, set aside a few minutes before you go to bed every night to tidy up this area. I use this time to make sure that the coffee table and end tables are clear of cups, papers, and other objects. Socks and shoes are carried to their proper homes. Toys and games are packed up and put away. Don't let your clutter and messes prevent you from relaxing in the future. Set the stage for more living to take place in this room the next time you want to use it.

Thursday at Work:
Working While at Work

If you work nine hours a day, five days a week, and take two
weeks of vacation a year, then you spend just over 2,200 hours a
year at your job. Add to that a wobbly desk chair and a wobbly
coworker and it feels like an even larger chunk of time. Since so
much of your life occurs while you're at work, there can be
hours or full days when you find it impossible to actually work
while you're in your office.

A few minutes goofing off each day, especially if shared with
coworkers, can actually improve your overall opinion of your
job. One of my favorite work moments was when the president
of the company I work for took the entire staff to play Whirly-
Ball[9] after a morning of heavy meetings. Riding around in bumper cars and hurling balls at one another was exactly what all of
us needed at the time.

Prolonged time wasting, however, is unacceptable. Taking
more time to perform a task than you should is also irresponsible. You are paid to do a job, and you should do it as efficiently
as possible. Remember that you work so that you can take care
of the things that matter most to you. Working makes it possible
to have a remarkable life.

Years ago, I was hired as an assistant-level content editor in
the public affairs department of an economic research firm. A
year and a half after that, I found myself in charge of the entire

department. More precisely, I was the department. I worked sixty to seventy hours a week just to keep emergencies to a minimum. I had never before experienced this kind of workload— I was constantly overwhelmed, and my office looked as if it had been hit by a tornado. My work life was a mess, I was expected to do the work of four people, and I burned out before I made it three years with the firm.

I describe the anxiety I experienced during this time as the Cloud of Doom. It followed me everywhere and weighed on me mentally and physically. I knew that I needed to manage my time better and have processes in place to handle my workflow, but I didn't know how to make that happen. After I resigned from the firm, I set out to find the answers and teach myself how to do my work as efficiently as possible. I never wanted to be in the position again where my work controlled my entire life, and I wanted to be rid of the Cloud of Doom.

If you're reading this section of the book, then my story might feel familiar to you. You are seeking ways to work with more focus, energy, and creativity so that you can get out from under your Cloud of Doom. The more productive you are at work, the less you have to think about work when you're not there (or the more time you have to think about it if your work is what matters most to you). Also, when you have strategies to complete your work, you're less anxious about what you have to accomplish.

Productivity and time management skills work hand in hand. If you're lousy at time management, you won't be productive. Conversely, if you aren't productive, you'll never master time management. To improve the way you work, you have to make a commitment to developing both of these skill sets.

Your Productive Day at Work

Imagine your ideal day at work. What milestones do you achieve? How much work do you finish? In the previous chapter, you identified your top priorities at work when you determined when you should say yes to an assignment and when you should say no (page 141). Within these priorities, what tasks do you need to accomplish to feel that you have had an incredibly productive day at work? What more do you want to do in addition to these minimum tasks?

Create an imaginary timetable and schedule all of the work you would do in a single day. Now take a realistic look at your timetable. Cross out any items that are impossible, but leave all of the items that you know you could achieve if you really pushed yourself. The amount of work left on your timetable is your first goal.

Tracking Your Productivity

Now that you have set your goal, it's time to identify your current level of productivity to see how much of an improvement you need to make. Unfortunately, this assignment will take you longer than the duration of this week, but I think that it's worth it. The data you gain will help you improve your productivity. I recommend using one of two methods to evaluate your performance. If you spend all of your work time behind a computer, it will be simplest for you to use a software program designed to track your work habits. Rescue Time (rescuetime.com) is a web-based program that you can use at no cost to better understand how you spend your time. Interact with the program and leave notes for yourself about the different kinds of work you're completing and what you're doing when you're not on your computer. After two weeks, access the program's reports of your work to see your workday highs and lows. The longer you chart your work, the more accurate the data.

If you don't have a desk job, use a notebook and stopwatch to record your workday in ten- or fifteen-minute intervals. Write down what you did throughout the course of your day, the same way a lawyer might record her time for billing purposes.

Simple notations on your tracking sheet like "Talking to Margot" and "Totally spacing out" will end up being worthwhile data points, so be sure to be honest and record what you're doing. Since this information is for your eyes only, there's no sense in fabricating your responses. The more honest you are, the more reliable your data.

When you start recording your actions, you're going to notice an immediate boost in productivity because the tracking process will make you more aware of how you're spending your time. This awareness may be all you need to reach your ideal level of productivity. Or after two weeks of tracking your work, you may notice a return to a work level similar to what it was before you started keeping records. If this is the case, the first days of data will be inconsistent with your regular behavior and you will want to throw out these data points.

Once you have enough data, analyze the information and

identify trends in your schedule. What hours of the day are you most productive? When do you find it hard to focus? Now you can start to adapt your workflow to better match your body's natural rhythms and improve your productivity.

Tracking your workflow also helps you to identify when you're poorly managing your time. If you're constantly late for meetings or missing deadlines, you can look at the data you've collected and identify why you're behind schedule. Do you have a coworker who constantly comes by your desk to gossip? Do you not have a plan in place to complete your work? Do you check your e-mail forty-two times in an hour? Does talking to a specific vendor get you so upset that it takes you five minutes or more to regain concentration after the call? Do you get off topic when you're on the phone? If you don't notice any trends yet, collect data for another week and be more specific in the notes that you're keeping.

Ways to Improve Your Productivity

There are almost as many productivity and time management strategies for you to choose from as there are books in the Library of Congress. The method I use is a hodgepodge of David Allen's method in *Getting Things Done*, consistent use of a project management program, self-discipline, motivation, and years of personal trial and error on systems of my own creation. The key is to find the system that works best for you.

To help you achieve your ideal productive day, work through the following steps. The first step is to understand what you do at work. If you took the time to track your workflow in the manner I previously discussed, then you have at least two weeks' worth of data explaining what it is you do during your workday. How many phone calls do you typically make? How many hours do you devote to research and writing? How many times do you sneak candy off the receptionist's desk?

Once you establish what it is you do, you will want to reference your ideal day that you created earlier based on your priorities and compare it to what you're actually doing with your time. What are the most important tasks you complete every day? What are the least important activities? Decide which tasks are top priorities, middle priorities, and low priorities. Next, you'll want to calculate how much time you're actually spending on the activities in each of these categories. Are you spending the majority of your time each day on the highest-priority items? If you're not, this could be a red flag that something is awry with your current productivity system.

When you analyzed your workflow, you identified the most important tasks you complete in a day. You should schedule yourself to work on tasks that require the greatest amount of time and energy during the times of the day when you are naturally the most productive. Midrange tasks should be scheduled for when you're still productive but have more interruptions or when your energy level starts to wane. Finally, those tasks that are good to do but you won't get fired for not finishing should be scheduled in your low periods of the workday. For instance, I'm most productive in the first three hours of my workday. If I start my day by checking e-mail or reading my favorite websites, I'm wasting my best writing time. So, unless I'm waiting on an important e-mail to direct my work for the day, I start writing right away and leave e-mail for when my productivity slows later in the morning. Most people notice a drop-off after lunch. If you notice these lulls in your productivity at a certain point in the day, you'll want to rearrange your schedule so that you only perform low-concentration activities then. I fill this time with returning phone calls, scanning and filing papers, checking e-mail, and reading items in my "Read Me" folder.

You can use a good ol' pen and paper to schedule your time or a computer-based program. I use a combination of both, using Google Calendar for my formal activities (meetings, appointments, etc.), a large paper calendar to set the Unclutterer writing schedule, a monthly notebook divided into forty-three sections that I use like a tickler file (similar to the folder system David Allen suggests in his book *Getting Things Done*), and a project management software program for my client-based work.

During your most productive times of the day, it is wise to hang a sign on the door to your office letting your coworkers know that you are working diligently toward a deadline and that you will not be available again until a specific time, except in cases of emergency. Not everyone may choose to respect this sign, but it will probably keep anyone who is simply coming by to chat from interrupting you. If you work in a cube, the sign idea probably won't work for you, but it never hurts to try.

If you have an assistant, instruct this person to be your communication gatekeeper for the whole day, or at least for the times when you need to be extremely focused. He should field all of your calls and e-mails and keep other employees and coworkers out of your office. Decide ahead of time what qualifies as an issue worthy of interrupting your focus, and have your assistant only disturb you in those situations.

Another way to see a boost in productivity is to be explicit about your work when interacting with your coworkers, boss, clients, and vendors. Wear your progress on your sleeve. Be open and honest and leave politics to those who work in the Capitol building. Notify the people who are dependent on you of your status, especially when a glitch or event changes your deadline. When you communicate well and manage others' expectations, you help them to better manage their time. When others do the same with you, you can better coordinate your schedule and efficiently complete your work.

Also, don't forget to use the techniques discussed for communicating by phone and e-mail. You've hopefully noticed a boost in your productivity already based on these improvements.

Stop Procrastinating

A good way to throw a wrench in your productivity is to start procrastinating. According to researchers at DePaul University, people procrastinate for three reasons:[10]

1. "Arousal procrastinators are thrill seekers who tackle projects at the last minute, pulling all-nighters at school and work.

2. Avoidance procrastinators habitually put off hard or boring tasks.

3. Decisional procrastinators are paralyzed by indecisiveness."

Knowing which kind of procrastinator you are can help you to stop procrastinating. If you're an arousal procrastinator, find another way to keep yourself entertained. Take up skydiving or downhill skiing—whatever it is that gives you a similar rush. If you're a decisional procrastinator, get a coach and start training yourself to be a better decision maker.

Avoidance procrastinators may find that continuing to use a timer will help with their productivity and focus. When you have a visual and auditory reminder that you have a set amount of time to complete a task, you can trick yourself into focusing on it. Also try these strategies for improving your productivity when you don't really want to work:

- Similar to what you might do when exercising, play music with a fast rhythm.

- If you drink caffeine, consume it in small, frequent amounts instead of just one large cup at the beginning of the day.

- Set time-specific goals in two-, five-, or ten-minute increments. Identify what you want to accomplish in a very short amount of time, and then set a timer and go for it.

- Isolate yourself. Remove the desire to procrastinate by not having any other options but to work.

- Acknowledge that you're procrastinating. Often, just realizing that you're putting something off is enough to get you working.

- Challenge a colleague to see who can get the most work done in a set time period.

- Ask someone to help you stay accountable. There are professional motivators who will call you once a day to see how you're doing, but a trusted and willing friend or coworker can do the same thing for free.

- If the task doesn't require much thought, listen to an audiobook while you work. Agree to only listen to the book when you're working on the project you don't want to do. This way, you'll be interested in hearing more of the story each time you take on the undesirable task.

Repercussions

Improving your focus and productivity at work is not all puppies and rainbows. Around the second week you will hit a wall of mental exhaustion. Pushing yourself to constantly work at your ideal level of productivity takes incredible energy, and you're going to feel exhausted if you are unaccustomed to working at your highest capacity for extended periods of time.

You will need to prepare for this event and act accordingly. Make room in your schedule for a few nights when you can head to bed early and give yourself the rest you need. Consider scheduling a massage or a weekend of doing nothing to help you recuperate.

In another week, you will become acclimated to the demands your mind is placing on your body and the sense of exhaustion should subside. If it doesn't, take a step back and evaluate whether you have unrealistic expectations of yourself. For most people, though, the mental exhaustion is temporary and your only long-term side effects will be improved focus and productivity.

Thursday Evening:
Your Home Office

In the Foundations chapter, I talked about how you achieve work-life symbiosis so that your work life and personal life exist together harmoniously. Without clutter and distractions, you can have a remarkable, rewarding life with the time and energy to pursue the things that truly matter to you.

There are days, weeks, and months, though, when the demands of one aspect of your life may play a larger part than you would like them to play. These discordant times are usually short-lived, expected, and, in the end, worth the additional effort. I'm certainly not a fan of having to work late or over the weekend instead of relaxing with my friends and family, but there are times when the additional work hours are inevitable. If I want to do my job well, occasionally I have to sacrifice some of my personal time to make that happen.

When these extra work hours appear on the schedule, it often means that you have to take work home and finish it there. Working from home can be a nice change of pace—you can work in your pajamas. Most productivity levels plummet, however, when the demands of your personal life are so physically close to you. It's hard to ignore your crying child when you are trying to finish a report that barely holds your attention in the office. It's difficult to turn off the Monday night football game when you have to reconcile a balance sheet.

In addition to bringing work home from the office, we also have need to do officelike work at home—bill paying, house managing, and keeping track of important documents. A designated space to take care of these needs is just as important as it is in a traditional office space. And, as we've already established, this space should not be your dining room table or in your bedroom.

Setting Up a Home Office or Workspace

Think of your home office as a formal workspace and make it suitable for long periods of work. Whatever equipment is on your desk in your work office should also exist in your home office. This may include a computer, monitor, keyboard, mouse, backup hard drive, printer, scanner, and telephone. You will need a filing cabinet and filing system, too, and you can find advice on how to set up this system in the Tuesday chapter. Also, make sure your seating is ergonomic so that you don't put unnecessary strain on your body. You'll take your work more seriously if you feel like you're at work.

To work effectively from home, you need to create a boundary between you and the rest of your house. You need to be able to focus and get your work done quickly so that you can return to your personal pursuits. A separate room for your office is ideal, but you also can create a portable office in an ottoman that has built-in storage or set up a rolltop desk in the corner of another room. If you go the nontraditional route, your biggest priority will be to stay away from the television and the main flow of traffic in the house.

Clear off your desk and return your materials to their storage locations when you are finished working. You want your workspace to be ready the next time you need to use it, and you won't want to look at the clutter from work when you don't have to. Additionally, any materials that need to go back to your off-site office or be put in the mail should be returned to your Reception Station so that you're ready to take them with you when you leave.

If you already have a home office and it needs to be uncluttered and organized, follow the advice in Monday's office section. Afterward, return to this chapter for more home office–specific suggestions.

Work from Home or Live at Work?

My husband likes to say that there is a misconception about people who work from home: People don't work from home; they live in their offices. Whether you're a full-time telecommuter or a parent who manages the house and children, being at home the majority of the time makes you feel like you are always at work.

My husband knows firsthand the truth of his statement because he has been telecommuting since 2000. When I started working from home in 2006, he was an incredible resource to me as I made this transition. We share an office (our desks are just seven feet away from each other), and I know I would have a much more difficult time working from home if he weren't here to keep me company.

Also, be aware that other people (friends, family) may have a harder time adjusting to your working from home than you do. They may assume that since you work from home you're free to run errands for them or that your work hours are flexible. Even if this is the case, it's best not to let other people know, at least initially. You want it to be clear that you are a professional and that your work is just as valuable as the work completed in more traditional office environments.

Here are just a few ways to establish a productive and enjoyable home working environment:

- *Create a workspace separate from everyone else in your home.* Establish a defined space that is just for your work. This may mean that you need two desks, two computers, and two phone lines in your home. Experience has taught me that when people share desks, one person always feels like they're invading the other person's space.

- *Know your UPS/FedEx/mail carrier's first name.* Delivery people are not accustomed to your being home during the day. Acquaint yourself with these people so that they will actually ring the doorbell and wait for you to answer the door when they have deliveries.

- *Make your office a place you want to be.* Similar to the advice I gave on Monday in the laundry section, you need to want to work in your space. Decorate the room, buy quality equipment and supplies, and have sufficient lighting for the needs of your work.

- *Purchase and use a good set of earphones.* Ultimately, there will come a time when you're in a productive zone and your roommate or spouse will decide to talk loudly on the phone or feel compelled to tell you about something funny. Music playing through the earphones allows you to tune out other conversations and also sends the message that you're not to be distracted (even if you're not actually listening to music).

- *Have a phone with a do-not-disturb button and forwarding capabilities.* Often, clients assume that because you work from home it's okay to call you at all hours of the night and on the weekends. If you worked in an office building, they would never have the expectation that you would answer your phone at dinnertime. When your workday is finished, press the do-not-disturb button on your work phone and let it ring straight to voice mail. That being said, if you take your dog for a walk around the neighborhood in the middle of the afternoon, it's best to forward your office phone to your cell phone so that you won't miss any important business.

- *Set strict office hours.* This is an important rule for you and for everyone else in your life. These boundaries keep you at your desk and productive throughout the day and also remind people that you are a professional. When you're done with work for the day, clear your desk, hit the do-not-disturb button on your phone, turn off the light, and close the door. If you're a parent who stays home to manage the house and take care of your children, schedule these work times to take place every day when the kids are napping or participating in a supervised activity.

- *Get ready at least a little bit every morning for work.* It's fun to work in pajamas, but it's not fun to let your hygiene go. Brush your teeth, shower, and put on something you won't be embarrassed to answer the door in when the UPS driver comes with a package. It helps your productivity when you feel more put together than you did when you were sleeping.

- *Take advantage of working from home.* Make yourself a nice breakfast or lunch in your kitchen. Work from your front porch on sunny afternoons. Throw a load of laundry into the washing machine before work, toss it in the dryer during lunch, and fold it at the end of the workday. Run to the post office when things are slow during your morning. Take advantage of the perks of working from home to remind yourself why you do it.

Managing Your Home

I like to think of home management in the same way I think of project management. And, really, they are the same thing. You have priorities—bill paying, home improvements, responding to mail, keeping your home insured—and you have tasks and deadlines related to all of these priorities. As a result, the same project management system I use for my job I also use to manage my home. My husband also has access to this system and we contribute to it, check off items, and make notes for each other to reference.

We also reduce paper clutter by using online banking access

with our financial institutions and online bill-paying services for
most of our utilities. Contact your bank and utility providers to
learn about these services for your specific needs. I also recommend Quicken's online software to track your expenses. The
service is free and has many security measures to keep your information private. One of the benefits of using all of these online services is that you can access your financial information
from anywhere. If your home is burglarized or if you're on vacation, you can still get to your important data.

Whether you work at home full-time or have an established
work space just for bill paying and filing important documents,
you'll find that having a set space for these activities helps your
overall work-life symbiosis.

Spring Cleaning Guide

Spring Cleaning for the Busy Person

- ☐ 1. Change your furnace filters.

- ☐ 2. Replace batteries in your smoke and carbon monoxide detectors and test them.

- ☐ 3. Check fire extinguishers.

- ☐ 4. Clean leaves and debris out of gutters.

- ☐ 5. Service lawn mower and prepare for summer use.

- ☐ 6. Store shoe tray, ice scraper, snow shovel, and winter items.

Kitchen

- ☐ 7. Scrub floors and counters.

- ☐ 8. Clean cabinets and drawers.

- ☐ 9. Inspect tableware for damage.

- ☐ 10. Clean refrigerator and freezer with a mild detergent.

- ☐ 11. Check expiration dates and dispose of expired food in refrigerator and pantry.

Bathroom

☐ 12. Toss expired makeup, liquids, and supplies.

Bedroom

☐ 13. Wash mattress pad, bed skirt, and comforter.

☐ 14. Wash heavy winter blankets and store in plastic until fall.

☐ 15. Clean heavy sweaters and put in storage with moth proofing.

☐ 16. Swap out cooler-weather clothing for warmer-weather clothing.

Dining room and living room

☐ 17. Move furniture and vacuum or sweep where furniture had been.

Home office

☐ 18. Move furniture and vacuum or sweep where furniture had been.

☐ 19. Clean desk.

☐ 20. Wipe down telephone.

Exterior spaces

☐ 21. Clean porches and patios.

☐ 22. Dust outdoor furniture and set out for use.

☐ 23. Rake leaves and branches from yard.

☐ 24. Hook up garden hoses.

☐ 25. Inspect pesticides and make sure none of the containers are leaking or expired.

Other

☐ 26. Properly dispose of expired medicines (page 61).

Spring Cleaning for the Dedicated Cleaner

☐ 27. Items 1–26.

☐ 28. Have furnace inspected.

☐ 29. Inspect and clean fireplace.

☐ 30. Vacuum out dryer hose.

☐ 31. Scrub lint trap on washing machine.

☐ 32. Inspect garage door opener and belt.

☐ 33. Inspect all floors and wax or steam clean.

☐ 34. Inspect walls for scuffs or damage.

☐ 35. Dust light fixtures and ceiling fans.

Kitchen

- [ ] 36. If necessary, defrost freezer.

- [ ] 37. Clean inside of oven, stove burners, and range hood.

Bedroom

- [ ] 38. Clean winter shoes and take repairs to cobbler.

Dining room

- [ ] 39. Clean sideboard and drawers.

Living room

- [ ] 40. Dust books and bookshelves.

Computers and electronics

- [ ] 41. Clean each item per manufacturer's instructions.

- [ ] 42. Go through digital files and organize data (page 84).

Exterior spaces

- [ ] 43. Replace doormats if needed.

Other

- [ ] 44. Clean and store winter sports equipment.

- [ ] 45. Have bicycles serviced.

- [ ] 46. Clean pet toys, food bowls, and accoutrements.

Spring Cleaning for the Overachiever

☐ 47. Items 1–46.

☐ 48. Inspect and service water heater.

☐ 49. Remove, clean, and store storm windows and replace with screens.

☐ 50. Wash exteriors and interiors of windows.

☐ 51. Wash curtains.

☐ 52. Schedule security system test.

☐ 53. Inspect all floors and wax or steam clean.

☐ 54. Take trash cans and litter boxes to self-service car wash and power wash.

☐ 55. Clean air vents.

Kitchen

☐ 56. Change filter in stove's range hood.

☐ 57. Clean exteriors of small appliances.

☐ 58. Pull refrigerator out from wall and wash floor underneath. Vacuum its coils.

☐ 59. Have knives professionally sharpened.

Bathroom

☐ 60. Launder shower curtain and replace liner if mildewy.

☐ 61. Clean showerhead.

Bedroom

☐ 62. Flip mattress, if recommended by the manufacturer.

☐ 63. Clean jewelry per manufacturer's instructions.

Dining room

☐ 64. Polish wood furniture.

☐ 65. Polish and/or dust display items.

Living room

☐ 66. Wash slipcovers and steam clean upholstered furniture.

☐ 67. Polish furniture and tables.

chapter 6

Friday

You have made it to the final day of the workweek. I commend you for all of the hard work you've done up to this point. In celebration, today's projects don't require any heavy lifting. Your Friday activities focus on clearing distractions from your schedule and work routines and relieving frustrations you might experience from living with people who aren't unclutterers. The work you'll complete this morning and afternoon is just as important as removing physical clutter, but you don't need to get your hands dirty to do it.

Friday Morning: Scheduling Strategies

In high school and college I didn't keep a calendar for anything except homework. My absurd philosophy was that if I didn't remember the event, it wasn't important enough for me to attend. This method worked (sort of) only because I was constantly surrounded by friends who did keep calendars and who made sure I was where I should be.

After I graduated and moved into an apartment on my own, I quickly realized that this method was one of the worst ideas I'd ever had. I kept missing appointments and showing up late. My friends had new jobs and were starting families; keeping track of where I needed to be wasn't a priority for them (and, let's be honest, it never should have been). Looking back, I'm shocked they tolerated my irresponsible behavior for so many years.

Keeping a calendar is beneficial not just to you but also to the people who depend on you. Trying to carry all of your appointments and obligations around in your mind creates stress. You have a looming feeling that you're always forgetting something or are on the verge of letting someone down. You might be able to remember a few important dates and times, but you'll never be able to remember them all.

Instead of juggling this information in your mind or carrying around a million little sheets of paper with notes scribbled on them, it's time to develop and use a reliable scheduling system to plan your day. Get rid of the stress, and free your mind to think about much more important things.

Traditional and Technical Scheduling Tools

Scheduling all the places you need to be and all the things you have to do can be an overwhelming activity the first time you do it. Keeping these commitments in one place may feel like an insurmountable task, which may be the reason you have been avoiding the activity.

As you begin this project, I want you to remember two things:

1. These are things you *get* to do. Having things on your schedule is a privilege. Not everyone is healthy enough to do so many things, or lives in a free society that allows them to. Except for a few situations, most items on your schedule aren't a life-or-death matter. You are choosing to participate in these activities.

2. It's okay to say no (see Wednesday for tips) and only do the things that truly matter to you.

First up, unclutter your schedule. Pick up the phone and respectively bow out of any commitments that are too much for you to handle and aren't related in any way to the things that matter most in your life (the things you put on your list of what matters most in the Foundations chapter). Take a stand and choose not to run for a third term as president of your home-owners' association or decline to volunteer for all ten of this summer's community theater bake sales. And, similar to what I mentioned on Wednesday, apply these techniques when saying no to an activity: Treat the request with respect, express appreciation for being considered, communicate any alternatives, and don't leave room for negotiation.

On the opposite side of this equation, if you're wishing you had more plans on your schedule, remind yourself about what matters most to you and schedule time for a related activity. Gaining control of your schedule is important to achieving work-life symbiosis and a remarkable life.

How you decide to keep track of your schedule is a matter of personal preference. If you are an auditory processor, you may prefer a digital calendar that has an alarm system that will automatically notify you (*ding!*) of upcoming appointments. If you are a kinesthetic processor, you may prefer to keep a handwritten calendar that involves the physical act of writing to create a schedule. If you are a visual processor, you might enjoy a combination of a digital and a handwritten method so that you can have different modes to see your plans. Whatever method you choose to implement, make sure that it is intuitive and convenient for your life and processing style, so that you will actually use it.

Digital Scheduling. Google Calendar (calendar.google.com) is currently the most ubiquitous and convenient digital scheduling program. It's free; allows you to share your schedule with friends and family in a weekly, monthly, or daily agenda format across multiple electronic devices; and has numerous notification capabilities (text message, e-mail, and desktop and smart phone pop-ups). You can even set the preferences to tell you what kind of weather to expect the day of an event. It syncs with Microsoft Outlook, iCal, and all iPods and is available in seventeen languages.

I especially like Google Calendar for event planning. If I decide I want to throw a dinner party, I can immediately access my husband's shared Google Calendar to see whether he has anything on his schedule. If he's free, I can send an invitation through the program to my friends and they can RSVP right back through the program. If my friends also use Google Calendar, they can even make their schedules available to me (it just says "busy" or "not busy"; it doesn't detail exactly what they're doing) so that I can figure out whether one day might be better than another for the party.

Paper Scheduling. At-a-Glance, FranklinCovey, Day-Timer, Day Runner, Filofax, and Planner Pads are all effective day-planning systems for keeping track of appointments by hand. The more compact the calendar, the easier it is to take with you. Unless you're in the habit of regularly scanning your calendar, you run the risk of "losing your life" if your paper planner is ever destroyed, stolen, or misplaced. However, it has the benefit of never needing an Internet connection or requiring a power cord to access the information inside of it.

I'm of the mind-set that you should be able to open up a planner and immediately figure out how to use it. If there are so many bells and whistles that you can't imagine utilizing the majority of the system, continue searching until you find the best match for you. Almost all of these systems have seminars, books, pamphlets, CDs, DVDs, or online training available to teach you how to use the product if you decide to go with a more complex product.

As I mentioned previously, I keep a large monthly calendar on my desk that I use to plan posts for Unclutterer.com. I like seeing the content for the site at once. I instantly know how long it has been since we ran a post about cable clutter or one on travel tips. Large monthly-view calendars are also nice for active families with young children so that everyone, including little eyes, can see when birthday parties, soccer practices, and music lessons are scheduled. Having children participate in creating the schedule also helps them to develop time management strategies of their own.

Keeping on Schedule

The great thing about a calendar is that all you need to do to maintain it is enter items immediately into it and reference it as often as necessary. Every time you make an appointment, record it on your calendar. Don't get into the habit of only recording some things or delaying putting things on the calendar, because you will inevitably forget and something will slip through the cracks. Get into the habit of checking your schedule to see what you need to do. As I sip my coffee in the morning, I like to review my schedule for the day and take a peek at what is on deck for tomorrow.

All that's left to do is use it.

You Say It's Your Birthday

Thanks to social networking sites like Facebook, it has become significantly easier to remember people's birthdays. A little present icon appears on your home page alerting you that five of your friends have birthdays on Tuesday. Grandma Jean and Uncle Phil probably aren't on Facebook, though, and they're the two people who will have hurt feelings if you forget their special days.

In programs like Google Calendar, you can enter birthdays as events and schedule them to recur every year. If you use a handwritten calendar system, you have to go through the process of transferring these dates from your previous calendar to your new calendar, which can take time and has more room for error.

If you like to use a paper calendar, try a completely different system that doesn't involve copying information every year. Buy an oversized index card file and tabs for each month of the year. On twelve index cards, write the months of the year and then list names and birthdates on the index cards for their respective months. Once a year, take the twelve index cards with you to a card shop and pick out birthday cards for everyone on your list. (I realize that this all-at-once method may seem a bit impersonal in its description, but that isn't the case in practice. When you're selecting the cards, you're still thinking about the exact person you want to give it to.) When you return home, file the index cards and the birthday cards behind their appropriate tabs in the index card file. On the first day of every month, write greetings, address envelopes, and put stamps on the cards. Put the cards in your Reception Station and put sticky notes on the envelopes to remind you when you should drop the card in the mail on your way to work.

On the same day that I buy all of the birthday cards, I also like to pick up ten to fifteen congratulations cards (these are good for anniversaries, new babies, new homes, weddings, and graduations), a couple of sympathy cards (which I hope not to have to use), ten to fifteen blank cards (half of them light-hearted and half of them more serious), and some extra birthday cards. I put a birthday card and two blank cards (one funny, one serious) in the glove box of my car as emergency backups (you would be surprised how handy these emergency cards have been over the years), and the remaining cards I file at the back of my index card file. I also buy a roll of a hundred Forever stamps at the post office and store them in the front of the index card file along with a nice black pen and a pad of sticky notes. Everything I need to send a card is all in one place and I never worry about forgetting someone's special day.

I need to give you a word of warning that buying all your cards for the year at one time is amazingly expensive. I didn't realize how much I spent on cards until the first time I did this activity. To help you get past the sticker shock, remember that you're saving yourself time and energy over the course of the entire year by doing this in one afternoon. Plus, the people in your life will truly appreciate the effort you made to remember their birthdays. You also can make your own cards or buy in bulk at a discounted rate from a card maker on Etsy (etsy.com).

Friday at Work: Routine Is Not a Four-Letter Word

The word *routine* can be a bad word in many offices. As employees, we're supposed to be constantly innovative and finding new ways to do things. However, many of us need to perform the same tasks on a regular basis as part of our job. If we create a new process every time we file a paper or insert our signature into an e-mail, we're wasting incredible amounts of time and energy.

Routines don't stifle your work, they improve it. Researchers at the University of California–Davis found that alternating between mindful work (work that requires intense thought and focus) and mindless work (routine activities that require very little processing power) enhances your efficiency and creativity.[11] Changing your focus to simple, routine tasks gives your brain time to mull over more taxing ideas in a relaxed state and gives you energy to propel yourself for your next round of difficult work.

Project Management

When it comes time to tackle the difficult work, being the lead on a project doesn't mean you have to exhaust yourself to achieve your goals. Understanding the science of deadline creation, project organization, expectation management, and the

tools available to you can make you the superstar project manager in your office. Even if you aren't spearheading the project,
you can become the employee in the office who always meets or
beats his deadlines.

These are the universal truths for why projects are not completed on time:

- Clients are never as prepared as they say they will be.
- Clients always change their mind.
- People always underestimate the amount of time it will take
  to do something.

Clients are never as prepared as they say they will be because
until they start a project, they have no idea what information to
gather. Clients always change their mind because it's not until
the project is under way that they are able to see that they initially gathered inaccurate information. Finally, people think
they work more quickly than they actually do, so estimates describe what they would like to do, not what they will do.

If you don't work directly with clients in your job, you can
easily replace the word *client* with *boss* and the statements will
likely be just as accurate. Inaccurate information and estimates
are inevitable, and your job as a project manager is to know
these truths and behave accordingly.

Every project begins in the same fashion: Someone says
they want a result and you become responsible for making it
happen. Your next step is to open the lines of communication
among everyone involved in the project. You need to know as

much as you can about what your client wants before making any promises, taking any actions, or setting any milestones. Although you might want to get to work immediately, the most productive thing you can do is fight that urge and simply gather data.

If you manage many projects, prepare yourself with a standard list of questions for your client. This form may be very simple (does the client wish to purchase product A, B, or C) or it may be more complex (a twenty-page questionnaire that you fill out during a face-to-face interview). These forms are rigid and lack creativity, but they streamline the process—helping you to prepare with the client and therefore minimize the damage from the first truth of project management.

Regardless of whether you have a list of questions or not, schedule an information-gathering session before you get deeply involved in your project. There should be no doubt about the expectations your client or your boss has for you.

Once you have adequate information to proceed, you can craft your project. The client will most likely determine the end goal for your work, and she may give you a deadline for when that work should be completed. You can proceed without a set deadline, but you must know the expected goal for the project before starting work.

Remember the third truth of project management: People always underestimate the amount of time it will take to do something. When it comes time to schedule milestones for the project, you have to remember this truth or you will miss your deadline. A good rule of thumb is to double everything up to a day. If you think something will take you two hours, plan for it to take four. If you think something will take you eight hours, plan for it to take sixteen. After eight hours, the double rule stops being as accurate. For projects that I estimate will take between one and five days, I just tag on an additional day. If someone says it will take him two weeks to complete a portion of the project, I add three additional days into the schedule.

I also have two schedules: the one my team works from and the one I give to the client. The schedule my team works from is based on the time estimations they gave to me, and the one the client sees is the buffered time line. On the off chance that the team meets their abbreviated schedule, the client is thrilled because the work comes in ahead of schedule and under budget (with fewer hours billed than expected). However, when the team runs behind their schedule, they still end up meeting client expectations.

During contract negotiations for this book, my editor asked whether I could have the manuscript to her by April 15. I multiplied 1,500 words (what I estimated I could produce in a day in addition to my other writing) by the number of weekdays between when I would sign the contract and April 15. Based on this number, I estimated that I would easily finish the book by March 31. I signed the contract and agreed to the editor's April 15 deadline. A few unexpected bumps came up during the writing of the book—I had to fly to Chicago for a quick trip, I had to write and plan a television appearance, and my mom was in a relatively bad car accident. (Unexpected events happen, and this is why work-life symbiosis is so important. There are times when you need to drop everything work related to take care of a personal matter.) These disruptions in the schedule ended up adding a week to the process and I didn't finish the text until April 7. Since this date was still well in advance of April 15, my editor was happy that I finished ahead of her schedule. I underestimated my time by a week on my schedule, but it didn't matter because I had the buffer.

Small Deadlines Are Better Than One Big Deadline

Specific, individual tasks and intermediate goals (which I also call milestones) move you through a project without making you feel overwhelmed. When you break the project into manageable chunks, you chip away at the overall project until there is nothing left to do. If you think of the project in the big-picture sense, the anxiety will cause you to procrastinate and you'll never achieve your goal. Focus on the small tasks, and you'll finish on time.

Prioritize your milestones in a way that naturally advances toward the final project goal. As long as you don't put the proverbial cart before the horse, you should be fine. If you have any questions about priorities, talk them through with a colleague or your boss. Once your milestones are set on your schedule, you can start to create to-do items to help you achieve your milestones.

All of the to-do items you create should be worded to reflect the exact work that needs to be completed. Don't write a vague statement like "Call Dan to learn about Client X" on your task list. Instead, be specific: "Call Dan in accounting at ext. 1234 on

Friday at one PM about the 2009 figures for Client X." Put this specific task into your calendar for Friday at one PM and don't think about it until then. If you call and have to leave a voice message, move the task to Monday at one PM and try again if you haven't heard back from him.

When Uncluttering Goes Too Far

There is a fine line between establishing specific tasks and over-managing your time and others' work. If you turn part of a project over to someone else on your team, let that person take full command of his or her portion of the project. Focus on planning your work and breaking that work into manageable pieces. It's best to stay away from control-freak territory.

Additionally, you don't want to waste too much time planning your work. Do what you need to do to guide your work, and then get working. A well-planned project is a thing of beauty, but your efforts need to be focused on finishing the project.

On Thursday, I talked about managing expectations and being explicit as essential components of overall productivity. This is especially true for the productivity of a project. Check in with your team members at least once a day to learn about their progress. The small accomplishments you make over the course of a project are also great talking points to share with your client. Your client can then use this information to plan her work and also to communicate with her boss.

If you're looking for specific project management tools, consider the following:

Paper Tools: Managing a project with a paper calendar is no different than scheduling any other activity. Write tasks and milestones on your calendar and check them off as you complete them.

Digital Tools: Most businesses I've worked for have had monolithic enterprise resource planning (ERP) systems that include project management modules. If your company has one, use it. If your company doesn't have an ERP, I recommend Basecamp. This system isn't fancy, but the basic features you need in a project management system are present (assignments to be done, time lines, client interaction, etc.). Other programs are 5pm, @task, Teamwork, or Wrike.

When You're Not in Control of the Project

Being a member of a team is just as important as being a project manager. Without you, the project will never be completed. In the same way your project manager sets the workflow for the entire project, you need to do the same for your piece of the project:

- Gather as much information as you can about the entire project

- Know the goal of your work as it relates to the overall project

- Create a realistic schedule

- Break your work into manageable chunks

- Prioritize your milestones

- Schedule specific tasks on your calendar

- Communicate with your project manager early and often

- Do your work

You may not always agree with the way a project is being managed or who is managing it, but in these situations you just have to suck it up. To be a productive and efficient member of the team, rise above the office politics, focus on your work, and do the work that you have been hired to do.

Learning from the Lazy

If you want to know how to do a boring task quickly and with minimal effort, seek out the wisdom of a lazy person. People who are lazy want to get the greatest amount of results with the least amount of effort. Some of the most productive, creative, and efficient employees I've encountered are really just lazy people who have found the easiest way to do their work.

This maxim is especially true in computer programming: The more basic the code, the faster it processes, and the less likely it is that bugs will disrupt or slow down the program. It's also true in terms of your home life: The less stuff you own, the less you have to clean, and the more time you have to do things beyond housekeeping.

Routines and Productivity

As I discussed on Tuesday, routines help you get the boring work out of the way so that you can spend more time on the things that truly matter to you. In the context of chapter 3, I was talking about your personal life, but the same is true in your work life. Daily routines help you to be organized and aware of your responsibilities and provide you with time to focus on the things that truly matter in your valuable work.

Establish routines for those actions that you repeat every day and/or once a week. You should have a start-of-the-workday routine, an after-lunch routine, and an end-of-the workday routine. Additionally, you may have routines for completing status reports or scanning and filing documents. Wherever a routine is possible, put one into place and get into the habit of doing it.

As an example, this is my end-of-the-workday routine:

- Review daily schedule and move any unfinished items to tomorrow's agenda

- Review tomorrow's schedule and mentally note any special circumstances

- Process any papers in inbox and scan and file documents

- Put away all office supplies and clear desk

- Push do-not-disturb button on office phone

- Swap external backup hard drive for new hard drive

- Power things off

- Return any kitchen items to kitchen

- Call it a day

There was a time when I had a sticky note with all of these tasks listed on it. The list on the sticky note helped me to remember the steps in my routine. After a few weeks, though, I no longer needed the list as a reminder and I tossed it into the shredder. If you're someone who works well from checklists, take the time to create a list for all your routines.

Routine Typing

I get a great amount of use out of a Mac program called Text-Expander (smileonmymac.com/textexpander), a software program that allows you to create keyboard shortcuts to insert previously drafted text into a document or e-mail. If you're on a PC, the program ActiveWords (activewords.com) has similar features, and both programs cost around $30.

I receive about two hundred e-mails a day and about a quarter of them require that I send a response. I like to include a signature with my e-mails that states my name and some contact information, but how much contact information depends on the person receiving my e-mail. I regularly use five different signatures. The most restricted includes only my name and website, and the least restricted includes very private information like my mailing address and direct telephone number. I have five signatures saved in TextExpander and keyboard shortcuts linked to each one. A shortcut command on my keyboard inserts hundreds of letters onto the page. I have shortcuts that automatically insert the Unclutterer submission guidelines for guest posts (335 words), the Unclutterer statement for reprinting of articles (177 words), and a list of staff telephone extensions (60 words). Ultimately, TextExpander and ActiveWords allow you to complete a long process in a matter of seconds. Speed up your workflow by using keyboard shortcuts for all of your routine typing and completely eliminate spelling errors.

Friday Evening:
Living with Clutterers

Now that most of the clutter and distractions are gone from your life, you may be noticing other people's stuff. If you live with someone or share an office space, that stuff might be physically close to you, or it could be a disorganized client, boss, or parent whom you are starting to notice and wish would change his ways. When this happens—and it will—you have to remember three things:

1. You cannot force someone else to become an unclutterer.

2. What matters most to you is different from what matters most to other people.

3. Being an unclutterer is not the only way to live.

As much as your new strategies and techniques have made a positive change in your life, don't think about your new way of living as being better than how other people choose to live their lives. Think of an uncluttered life as being easier for *you*.

You've chosen to acquire organizing skills, clear clutter from your life, and seek out a remarkable existence focused on what matters most to you. These are life-improving choices, but ones that you have chosen to make. Respect that not everyone comes to this same conclusion or is even aware that it's an option.

Wasting time and energy stressing out about other people having clutter in their lives only adds clutter to your life.

You can lead by example and talk to others about the benefits you've gained by becoming an unclutterer, but you can't scream, nag, or bully them into making a change. However, you can peacefully coexist with them.

Ten Tips for Living with a Clutterbug

1. Know what you're getting into before living with someone else. When considering moving in with someone (in a romantic relationship or otherwise), a person's level of order and cleanliness should be part of the equation if this is really important to you. If you can't stand clutter, don't move in with someone who loves it. You have a choice, and you can choose *not* to live with this person.

2. Communication is your best friend when living with a clutterbug. If you're already in a living arrangement and are uncomfortable with your partner/roommate/child's level of order, you need to have a conversation with that person. Yelling and passive-aggressive behavior aren't productive and damage the relationship. Having a calm, sincere, and respectful conversation, however, has the possibility of yielding powerful results.

3. Have the conversation in a public place if you're likely to start yelling. Most people don't yell in a nice restaurant no matter how heated a discussion they are having.

4. Establish ground rules for how you will talk to each other about clutter and disorganization. My favorites are No nagging, No backpacking (bringing up topics that have previously been resolved), and The real problem must be the topic of discussion (not whatever unrelated thing set you off).

5. Review your routines and processes with the other person to make sure they are aware of systems you've put in place to deal with messes before they happen. Your roommate might not know why you've put a shredder by the front door or that you like the counters to be clear of dirty dishes to keep bugs and pests out of your home. What is obvious to you may not be obvious to someone else. Don't be condescending or judgmental when explaining these systems; just talk about them.

6. Take care of the mess yourself. If something is really bothering you and it only takes a few seconds to fix, then by all means take care of it. I'm not suggesting that you become a maid and constantly clean up after the people in your home, but you can lend a hand once in a while. It's a difference of five seconds fixing a problem versus two hours being pissed that there is a pair of dirty socks on the living room floor. Don't clutter up your emotions if you don't have to.

7. Most people overestimate their contributions to work done around the house. We focus on what we're doing, attach a sense of worth to it, and assume what the other person is doing isn't as valuable. Make a list of all that you do in a day and ask your roommate to do the same. He or she might not know how much you actually do, and vice versa. In keeping with the no-backpacking rule, be sure to get rid of the lists after your discussion.

8. Walk through your home and talk about what you imagine for each space. Allow everyone to voice his or her ideas equally. How do you use the spaces and what do you need to do to keep these areas maintained? Make chore lists and create routines with one another.

9. Motivate instead of complain. Use audio or visual cues like those that were discussed on Tuesday to increase motivation. Let others see the benefits in your life from being uncluttered.

10. Seek outside help if you are having significant difficulty with your living arrangement. This help can be in the form of a professional organizer, a couples counselor or therapist, or maybe a cleaning service.

chapter 7

The Weekend

Sit back, put your feet up, and rest awhile. You've made it to the weekend. Enjoy the uninterrupted personal time that you have until you return to work on Monday. If you keep up your regular routines at home, your weekend should be relatively free of housework. Want to go for a long run? Do it. Want to hear your favorite band play live? Go to the show. This is when you can more deeply explore the "life" component of your work-life symbiotic plan.

When you started this transformation, you listed the things in your life that matter most to you. Spend time with your friends and family, travel, explore your spirituality—focus on whatever was on your list. Live your remarkable life, and continue to develop the life that you want for yourself.

Taking Care of Yourself

For a recent birthday, my mother-in-law gave me a gift certificate for a massage at a nearby spa. I immediately scheduled an appointment and was able to have a massage that very day.

When the massage therapist was working on the muscles in my back, I had to fight the urge to scream. I knew that she was barely touching me, but my muscles were so tense that even the lightest touch inflicted pain.

At the end of the session, I felt significantly better than before, but I knew I still had knots in my neck and back. The massage therapist was very good at her job, but she only had an hour to undo the damage that I had inflicted on my muscles for years. I decided that even though it was expensive, I was going to budget for and schedule a monthly appointment to have a massage. Knots in my muscles give me headaches, cause back pain, and make it harder to do my job. Plus, when I'm relaxed, I move more smoothly through every aspect of my life.

Ever since, I've kept that monthly appointment and my only regret is that I didn't start the habit earlier. I get a monthly massage for the same reasons that I go running every day, eat well, sleep on a set schedule, and spend fifteen minutes each morning just sitting in silence. If you don't take care of yourself, you can't function at your highest potential. When you don't take care of yourself, you ultimately let everyone else down, too. You don't have to get a monthly massage if it doesn't help you relax, but you should find what helps you recharge and commit to doing it on a regular schedule.

Preparing for the Worst

No matter how much we would like to pretend it's not possible, emergencies can strike at any time. The more organized you are, the easier it is for you and those closest to you to handle the aftermath and rebuild.

Take an inventory of everything in your home and store this data securely online. An emergency can be traumatizing and you may forget a good portion of the things you owned. Having a record of everything removes the margin of error when reporting the losses to your insurance company. Be sure to remove items from your inventory when you get rid of them and add items when you bring new things into your home.

Have your photographs and home videos digitized and backed up securely online. A friend of mine lost all of his pictures in Hurricane Katrina and says they are greatly missed.

Finally, if you're over eighteen, you should have a Last Will and Testament. Go to a civil lawyer and have one drafted immediately if you don't already have one. Store it according to your lawyer's recommendations.

Hobbies and Making the Most of Your Personal Time

There are hundreds of books and resources available on the topic of breaking up with a love interest. There are even ones exploring the topic of breaking off a toxic friendship and dumping bad business relationships. But until now there was absolutely nothing out in the ether on how to kick a hobby to the curb.[12]

Do you consider yourself a tennis player, but the last time you touched your racket was when Bill Clinton was president? Do you like the idea of being a scrapbooker but have never made a complete scrapbook? Are you keeping canvases for masterpieces you may one day paint, yet all of your paints are dried and your brushes are deteriorating? Is your guitar missing strings and in a case at the back of a closet? Do you have areas of your home set aside for or filled with stuff related to a hobby that you spend less than ten hours on a year?

If you answered yes to any of these questions, you are just not that into your hobby.

It can be difficult to admit, but if you're not averaging at least an hour per month pursuing a hobby, it's time to let it go. The space you're sacrificing in your home is too valuable to store things you don't use, even if you don't have storage issues. Every time you walk past what you're not using, you may think, "I wish I had more time to do X." You don't need that guilt. If it were really important to you, you would pursue it.

Five Steps for Deciding If Now Is the Time to Ditch Your Hobby

1. Identify all of your hobbies and all of the things associated with them in your home, garage, and office. You may benefit from collecting these items and laying them all out in your front yard or an open space in your home to see how much space you're sacrificing.

2. List all of these hobbies and then estimate how much time you've spent pursuing each of them in the last twelve months. Be honest with yourself.

3. The materials for any hobby you spent ten hours or less on in the last year should immediately be moved out of your

home. Pack up the equipment and head to a used sports equipment store or an appropriate charity. If the hobby stuff is valuable, photograph it and list it for sale on a site like eBay or Craigslist.

4. The space taken up by a hobby's equipment versus the time you spend on that hobby should be carefully reviewed, too. If you went camping one day last year, you would have spent twenty-four hours on this hobby. However, is one day of camping worth all of the space used to store your tent, sleeping bag, and all other accoutrements? On the flip side, if you spent one Friday night a month last year playing bridge with friends and averaged about two hours of playing time a sitting, it's probably worthwhile to hold on to a small deck of cards.

5. Any hobby you spent more than twenty-four hours a month on should also be reviewed. You may realize that your hobby is taking up so much time and space that you're neglecting more important things in your life, like time with your spouse or children. It's okay to break up with these hobbies, too. In most cases, however, you probably have a healthy relationship with your active hobbies and you'll decide to keep up with them. You will still want to evaluate how much stuff you have for them. If you have more supplies than you could use in a lifetime associated with that hobby, it's time to weed through the collection of stuff. My rule of thumb for intense hobbies is that you should never have more supplies than you could possibly use in a year—and you should have less than that if you can manage. If you have more yarn than you could knit in a lifetime, it's time to let some of it go.

There is a caveat to my assumption that you're just not that into your hobby—the truth may be that you really like your hobby, but somewhere along the way you misappropriated your time and let it fall by the wayside. Instead of making chairs in your woodworking studio, you've been watching television. If this is the case, make new priorities and recommit to your hobby. Turn off the television and head to your studio. Decide to reevaluate that hobby in six months. If in six months, however, you're still watching television, then it's time to admit that watching television is your hobby, not woodworking.

Vacation and Travel

Exploring the world, or even just a little corner of it, might be on your list of what matters most. It's certainly on mine. I want to eat Indian food in India, run a marathon from Athens to Marathon, and walk part of the Great Wall of China. I may not get to every destination on my list, but I'm definitely going to try.

Traveling can be frustrating at times, especially when unexpected events throw your plans for a loop. But one or two disruptions are easy to forget over a couple of Mai Tais on a tropical beach. Being prepared and organized with your plans can reduce these disruptions, and it's helpful to spend some time on the things you can prepare for.

Research your destination before you travel. If you're going to another country, learn where the U.S. embassy is located. Find online reviews of lodging options and make reservations based on this information. Learn local tipping customs. Con-

firm when places are open so that you don't miss out on a must-
see stop. Check out SeatGuru (seatguru.com) to make sure you
get a good seat on the plane. Like with all project management,
start by collecting data.

Make a packing checklist and pack lightly. A packing checklist reduces the likelihood that you'll forget something important. If I'm traveling for more than four days, I expect to do
laundry while I'm traveling. A small bottle of detergent to wash
clothes in the hotel bathtub or laundry facilities takes up significantly less space in your bag than three weeks worth of
clothes. You can also pack clothes that are all of the same color
palette so that you can mix and match parts of outfits.

Instead of carrying purchased items the whole route of your
trip, mail purchases back home as you're on your journey. Additionally, you can mail yourself items to pick up at hotels along
the way.

Unpack your suitcase immediately after you return home.
Don't let a bag sit for days after a vacation.

Let your luggage work double duty. If your luggage doesn't nest
smaller pieces inside of it, use your empty luggage to store out-of-
season clothing or linens when you're at home.

Being a Social Butterfly

You shouldn't have to wait for the weekend to have a social life—you can have one during the workweek, too. Just because you have to get up and go to work the next morning doesn't mean you have to be a homebody Sunday through Thursday. I'm obviously not advocating that you take up a heavy partying habit that jeopardizes your job. But part of work-life symbiosis is seamlessly moving between your work life and your personal life. You can enjoy a Wednesday evening out with friends as much as you would spending time with them on a Saturday afternoon (which I also think you should do). And if you're like me and work from home, getting out of the house and going to a social event is a requirement for keeping your sanity during the workweek.

One of my biggest complaints about adulthood is that it's difficult to simply hang out with friends. In high school, you could call up your friend and say, "Hey! A bunch of us are hanging out at Kara's place. Stop by if you want to hang out." No one scheduled "hanging out" on their calendar. No one knew at the start of the night what might transpire by the end of the night. And no one ever left at eight thirty, tapping at her watch, saying she had an early day tomorrow.

When I graduated from college, I was completely unprepared for having to schedule time to hang out with my friends. The first time one of my friends told me that she had to check her calendar to see when we might be able to grab lunch together, I laughed so hard I made myself cry. Oh, to have so few responsibilities that we could hang out whenever we want!

Review your list from the Foundations chapter that identifies the things that matter to you most. Is spending quality time with friends and family on your list? What else is on your list? Schedule the time now to live the remarkable life you desire.

- *Don't turn your back on your routines.* A little time every day spent on basic routines will provide you with more time in your schedule to pursue the things that truly matter.

- *Plan at least one social event a week.* Make a date with your friends or loved ones and keep that obligation. If the people in your life are really a priority, then you need to respect the time you spend with them. Say no to less important requests for your time and keep your date.

- *Plan at least one stay-home event a week.* If you're already a social butterfly, make a commitment to staying home at least one evening a week and taking care of yourself.

- *Keep a list of things you want to do, and do them.* Have a list on your smart phone or carry a small notebook with you, and record things you want to do. I have lists of wines I want to try, new restaurants that are getting good buzz, day trip locations, bike trails I've discovered, and dozens of other things that have caught my attention. When you're organized and focused on what really matters, you'll never have the opportunity to say, "I'm bored."

- *Pay money to take a class.* When you spend money on a class, you're more likely to make a commitment to attending it. If you want to have more variation in your meal plan, take a cooking class at your local cooking school to give you ideas and confidence. If you have always dreamed of going to Rome, sign up for Italian language classes at the local community college to get you prepared. If you wish that you and your significant other would go out dancing, take a ballroom dance class together. If finances are tight, look for free classes listed in your newspaper and make the extra effort to attend.

- *Stop making excuses.* You can come up with reasons for why you can't do something until you're blue in the face. Instead of wasting the energy coming up with those reasons, use that same energy to find ways to make it happen. You'll be surprised by your ingenuity.

chapter 8

Celebrating and Maintaining Your Success

You successfully purged your life of clutter. You've become a more efficient, productive, and focused worker. You've created a symbiotic relationship between your work life and your personal life. You're focused on what truly matters. You've found that simplicity is truly revolutionary. The hard work is behind you, and all you need to do from this point forward is focus on maintaining your uncluttered life.

You can maintain an uncluttered state by continuing to stay focused on what matters most to you, remembering the motto *A place for everything and everything in its place,* diligently asking questions about your things, and every day choosing to get rid of the distractions that get in the way of a remarkable life.

Keep up with the routines you established in your home and office to prevent clutter from sneaking back into your life. Since your priorities change with time, you may need to repeat specific uncluttering projects if the need arises. When you pick up this book each fall and spring to use the cleaning guides, review the rest of the book for a boost of inspiration. It's nice to remember how far you've come.

You really have achieved an incredible amount of success:

- You went on a sentimental journey and said good-bye to emotional clutter.

- You transformed your wardrobe and office into organized spaces that reflect who you are and help you to be more efficient.

- You created a Reception Station to keep clutter from entering your home and quickly launch you into the world when you need to leave.

- Your bathroom is now a place where you can find what you need when you need it. And your guests can find and make use of the things that you have realized you don't want.

- You no longer have stacks of paper rising like stalagmites on the horizontal surfaces in your office, and you have a Personal Data Collection worthy of praise.

- You do chores for only thirty minutes a day, five days a week, to keep your personal life and home free of messes.

- You have fall and spring cleaning lists to prepare you for those times when you need to give your home a little extra love and attention.

- You turned your bedroom into a place for rest and rejuvenation and determined how much sleep you need to function at your best.

- You streamlined your commute so that you always arrive at work on time.

- You improved your communication to make you more productive in the workplace.

- Your kitchen now runs like a well-oiled machine, and you can enjoy meals at the dining room table.

- Your living room has many purposes, but that didn't stop you from turning it into a place where you can do some remarkable living.

- You imagined your ideal level of productivity and worked assiduously to make it happen.

- You created a home office that helps to make your work-life symbiosis a reality so that you never have to feel like you live in your office.

- You implemented a schedule so that nothing slips through the cracks and you show up to the events that you want to attend.

- You are following new work routines that have increased the speed at which you perform your repetitive tasks.

- You have learned to live with others who may not be as uncluttered as you are.

- You're benefiting from your uncluttered life and taking full advantage of your personal time.

Give yourself a virtual gold star, because a real gold star would just be clutter.

Notes

1. Dean Ornish, MD, et al., "Intensive Lifestyle Changes for Reversal of Coronary Heart Disease," *Journal of the American Medical Association* 280, no. 23 (December 16, 1998): 2001–7.

2. James Wolf, "The Power of Touch: An Examination of the Effect of Duration of Physical Contact on the Valuation of Objects," *Judgment and Decision Making* 3, no. 6 (2008): 476–82.

3. Penelope Trunk, "Neatness Counts: A Messy Desk Can Hurt Your Career," *Penelope Trunk's Brazen Careerist* blog, January 6, 2003.

4. Larissa Larsen, "Plants in the Workplace: The Effects of Plant Density on Productivity, Attitudes, and Perceptions," *Environment and Behavior* 30, no. 3 (May 1998): 261–81.

5. Jon Peddie Research, "The Multiple Display Market and Consumer Attitudes," http://jonpeddie.com/special/MultDisp.shtml

6. "Tuesday at 11:45 Is Most Stressful Time of the Week, Survey Suggests," *Telegraph*, April 7, 2009.

7. "Some Thread Counts Are Bogus," *Consumer Reports,* January 2008.

8. You can see an image of our home art gallery system online at unclutterer.com/2007/07/16/gallery-hanging-systems-can-solve-artwork-clutter/.

9. WhirlyBall is a game that combines basketball, lacrosse, and bumper cars. Players are divided into two teams of five and have to stay seated in their WhirlyBug (bumper car) during the game. Whichever team has the most points at the end of fifteen minutes wins the game.

10. J. Peder Zane, "Why We Procrastinate," *News and Observer,* April 15, 2008.

11. Kimberly D. Elsbach, "Enhancing Creativity Through 'Mindless' Work," *Organization Science,* July–August 2006.

12. This specific text originated as a post I wrote for Unclutterer.com in April 2008.

Resources

Chapter 1: Foundations

    Scan My Photos (scanmyphotos.com)

    Pixily (pixily.com)

Chapter 2: Monday

    Style Statement by Danielle LaPorte and
        Carrie McCarthy

    Best Buy (bestbuy.com)

Chapter 3: Tuesday

    Evernote (evernote.com)

    Google Desktop (desktop.google.com)

    Copernic Desktop (copernic.com)

    Online storage options: Mozy (mozy.com), Amazon S3
        (aws.amazon.com/s3/), Box (box.net), and
        Carbonite (carbonite.com)

Chapter 4: Wednesday

Google Maps (maps.google.com)

eRideShare (erideshare.com)

Slug lines (en.wikipedia.org/wiki/Slugging)

iTunes (apple.com/itunes)

Audible (audible.com)

Library audiobook search (search.overdrive.com)

Kindle (amazon.com/kindle)

Sony eBook Store (ebookstore.sony.com)

Stanza app for iPhone (lexcycle.com)

Instapaper (instapaper.com)

Campfire (campfirenow.com)

Skype (skype.com)

RSS feed readers: Google Reader (reader.google.com),
    NewsGator (newsgator.com), Ensembli (ensembli
    .com), and Bloglines (bloglines.com)

Yahoo! Pipes (pipes.yahoo.com)

Toastmasters (toastmasters.org)

Tupperware (tupperware.com)

Rubbermaid (rubbermaid.com)

Freecycle (freecycle.org)

Still Tasty (stilltasty.com)

Chapter 5: Thursday

Elfa (containerstore.com/elfa/index.jhtml)

Netflix (netflix.com)

Rescue Time (rescuetime.com)

Getting Things Done by David Allen

Quicken online (quicken.intuit.com)

Chapter 6: Friday

Google Calendar (calendar.google.com)

Paper planners: At-a-Glance (ataglance.com),
FranklinCovey (franklincovey.com), Day-Timer
(daytimer.com), Day Runner (dayrunner.com),
Filofax (filofax.com), and Planner Pads
(plannerpads.com)

Project management software: Basecamp
(basecamphq.com), 5pm (5pmweb.com),
@task (attask.com), Teamwork (twproject.com),
and Wrike (wrike.com)

TextExpander (smileonmymac.com/textexpander)

ActiveWords (activewords.com)

Chapter 7: The Weekend

eBay (ebay.com)

Craigslist (craigslist.org)

Seat Guru (seatguru.com)

Acknowledgments

Agreeing to write a book is the scariest thing I have ever purposefully done. I understand this sounds absurd, especially coming from a woman who introduces herself at cocktail parties as a writer, but I would be lying if I said that I wasn't terrified when I started this adventure. Now that the book is in print and the process of creation is behind me, I know that I survived this roller-coaster ride because of the amazing people who were there for the journey.

I would first like to thank the readers of Unclutterer.com. Your continuous pursuit of remarkable living is powerful and inspiring. I love showing up to work every day knowing that I get to interact with such an inquisitive and exceptional group of people. I am blessed to be able to work for all of you.

This book would never have happened if it weren't for Cara Bedick, my superstar editor at Simon Spotlight Entertainment. I am awed by your vision, talent, and passion. You are a truly gifted editor. I am also indebted to my brilliant team at Simon

& Schuster, including Jen Bergstrom, Tricia Boczkowski, Kristin Dwyer, Michael Nagin, Lisa M. Robinson, Diane Hobbing, Mark Watkinson, Jaime Putorti, and Jessica Chin.

I cannot imagine surviving this process without my power-house agent Courtney Miller-Callihan at Sanford J. Green-burger Associates. You are a wise, wise woman. I have infinite respect for the extraordinary work you do. Thank you for seeing the world through my eyes and being a trusted adviser and friend. My only hope is that my strange obsession with deadlines, knitting socks in bars, *Little Girl Lost*, and trying to comprehend the publishing industry brought you many hours of entertainment.

This book wouldn't have been possible without the love, support, and patience of my husband. The life I now lead and passionately enjoy would not exist if you hadn't sat down with me on that spring afternoon to talk about my stuff. You are my inspiration, my best friend, and my catalyst. This book is dedicated to you.

Special recognition goes out to my mother, father, and brother for keeping me levelheaded and encouraging me no matter what ridiculous schemes I plan. Most important, thank you for putting up with me when I didn't know how to do anything but make a mess.

Thank you David Allen for contributing the Foreword and for your inspiring productivity and organizing insights. You are generous with your wisdom.

Earnest applause for my cheerleading squad: Stephen and Krystal Slivinski, Amanda Boatright, Kara Heitz, David Sylvester, Jason Ramirez, Katie Doland, the extended Rooney and Doland clans, Laurie Perry, Kim O'Donnell, Leo Babauta, Jonathan Fields, Gretchen Rubin, Melissa Parrish, and my Friends at Herndon Friends Meeting. You gave me guidance, support, laughter, and love when I needed them most.

My heartfelt appreciation goes out to Matt Niemi, Glen Stansberry, Lauren Halagarda, Monica Ricci, Geralin Thomas, Holly Becker, Gary DuVall, Gregory Go, Sue Brenner, and Danielle LaPorte for coming to my rescue and producing content for Unclutterer.com when my brain could think of nothing but this book. Also to Ralph Loglisci, Susan Martin, and Brian Kieffer.

My sincerest gratitude goes to the Unclutterer.com and Dancing Mammoth staffs for all of your hard work, dedication, and ability to put up with my bizarre ramblings and requests. I couldn't ask for better dance partners. And thanks to Jerry Brito for assigning me that first Unclutterer article in 2007, which, if memory serves me correctly, was about organizing shoes.

Finally, I would like to thank coffee (yummy, yummy coffee) and my trusty MacBook for seeing me through this unbelievable experience.